Effective Strategies to Leverage Change, Thrive, Innovate, and Lead in Tomorrow's World

THE
POWER
OF
CHANGE

MELISSA LEICH

Published by Growfused Press

Every effort has been made to obtain permission for material throughout the book. If any required acknowledgements have been omitted, or any rights overlooked, it is unintentional. Please notify the publisher of any omission, and it will be rectified in future editions.

Cover design by Alexander Liang
Interior design and formatting by Eros Martinuzzi

Trade Paperback ISBN: 978-3-9505462-0-0
eBook ISBN: 978-3-9505462-1-7

" The world as we have created it is a process of our thinking. It cannot be changed without changing our thinking."

~ Albert Einstein

A Gesture of Deep Appreciation

To everyone who takes the journey through these pages, thank you. Your quest for knowledge, understanding, and growth is the very reason these words were penned.

To my friends and colleagues, whose unwavering support and belief in my vision have been the foundation upon which this work stands. You've been my sounding board, my safe haven, and the source of countless inspirations.

To the countless individuals I've met along my journey who've shared their stories of change, resilience, and adaptation. This book, in many ways, is a tribute to all of you.

And lastly, to the unsung heroes behind the scenes—the editors, researchers, designers, and many others whose invaluable contributions transformed an idea into tangible work in your hands.

May the insights you discover in these pages push you forward, inspire change, and enrich your journey through life. Here's to embracing the power of change!

How to Use The Power of Change: Effective Strategies to Leverage Change, Thrive, Innovate, and Lead in Tomorrow's World

Navigating the landscape of tomorrow demands more than a roadmap—it requires a flexible strategy, the resilience to stay the course, and the insight to embrace transformation. *The Power of Change* has been crafted to guide you as you work through the inevitable changes in life.

But how do you maximize the value of these pages? Here's a brief guide:

1. Begin with Openness: Reading this book demands an open mindset. Embrace the content with curiosity and allow the insights to resonate with your unique experiences.

2. Progress Sequentially or Jump Around: While the book flows logically from understanding change to building resilience, you might be drawn to specific chapters based on current challenges or interests. It's designed to either be read from cover to cover or to focus on chapters that resonate most at the moment.

3. Engage with the Exercises: After reading and digesting each chapter, don't rush past the exercises. They're crucial. Think of them as mini-workshops, carefully designed to spark introspection, catalyze action, and help you transform theory into practice. Taking notes, sketching out thoughts, or even discussing them in group settings can magnify their impact.

4. Reflect on the Case Studies: Real-world examples bring to life the concepts presented. Take a moment to reflect on each case study. How do the challenges and solutions resonate with your own experiences? What might you have done differently? These stories offer both insight and inspiration, showcasing tangible applications of the strategies discussed.

5. Take the Strategies to Work: When envisioning the regular mentorship-style meetings mentioned in the text, customize them to fit your needs. Perhaps you'd prefer a comfy ambiance or a more formal setting; the key is to ensure they facilitate growth, learning, and continuous achievement.

6. Keep The Power of Change Accessible: This isn't a book you'll read once and set aside. As you journey through various stages of change, different sections will gain relevance. Keep it within arm's reach, whether for a quick consultation or a deeper dive.

7. Seek Support and Share Insights: While personal introspection is invaluable, dialogues can amplify understanding. Discuss concepts with peers, share your revelations, or even form a reading group. The richness of this book grows when its ideas are shared, debated, and reshaped in the crucible of collective insight.

Remember, *The Power of Change* isn't just a guide—it's an invitation to craft a future where adaptability fosters growth. Embrace it, and take steps towards becoming your most dynamic and resilient self.

TABLE OF CONTENTS

Introduction

In the quest for personal and organizational growth, it's easy to become entangled in stressors and complexities. Information overflows, deadlines loom, and the urgency of constant accessibility complicates our lives. Yet, beyond the chaos lies a striking paradox: the very elements that complicate our journey can also catalyze our greatest transformations. This book is an invitation to confront this paradox. Here, we examine the elements of change in a rapidly moving world and find our innate capacity to adapt, grow, and, ultimately, thrive.

Let us ask ourselves: If stress is inevitable, shouldn't we use it to our advantage? After all, it's only by embracing challenges and transcending them that we truly gain confidence and contentment. From discovering the psychology behind our perceptions of change to optimizing how we function in the AI-driven world, *The Power of Change: Effective Strategies to Leverage Change, Thrive, Innovate, and Lead in Tomorrow's World* is a comprehensive guide and a proactive dialogue on managing change.

Whether you're leading a high-performance team, grappling with the ethical implications of AI, or seeking to fine-tune your mental resilience, this book goes beyond the formalities. It's an informal meet-up in a comfy atmosphere where your goals, concerns, and aspirations are the focus. It's a space where vision meets action, where theoretical meets practical, and where the learning never stops. Each chapter includes exercises and real-world case studies to help spark introspection and catalyze tangible changes. These aren't just facts and figures thrown at you; they're intellectual stimulants geared to foster positive dialogue. And let's not forget, this isn't just about navigating change; it's about channeling its force to move ourselves and our organizations forward.

So prepare to dig deep. Formulate goals, and anticipate the goals that the world—your mentor in this journey—might have for you. *The Power of Change* isn't just another book; its value unfolds in the reciprocity between the reader—you—and its contents.

The future is not set in stone; it's dynamic, just like the strategies and insights packed into these pages. Embrace the transformation. Maneuver through the uncertainty. Relish the thrill of what lies beyond the horizon. Welcome to *The Power of Change*. Let's embrace these ever-evolving landscapes together and uncover the unparalleled growth and contentment they hold.

CHAPTER 1

Understanding Change

I n the first chapter, 'Understanding Change,' we invite you on
an engaging exploration into the essence of change, a constant and dynamic force in our world. We'll look into the
complexities of change, examining its role and influence in our
lives and society. This journey is more than just an academic
study; it's an opportunity to experience the impact of change on
both personal and collective levels.

Prepare to be immersed in a narrative that spans historical periods, from the Industrial Revolution to the digital era, and discover how these major shifts have shaped civilizations. We'll link
these broad changes to the subtle yet significant transformations
in our individual lives, exploring how our dreams and perspectives evolve in response to the world around us. This chapter is
not merely an introduction; it's an engaging invitation to perceive change as an active, influential force in every aspect of our
lives.

Gear up for a thought-provoking experience that encourages
questioning and offers a fresh perspective on the world. 'Understanding Change' sets the stage for an enlightening and transformative journey into understanding change, promising to
deepen your appreciation of its significance in shaping our world

and ourselves. This is not just the start of a chapter; it's the beginning of an insightful exploration into the dynamics of change.

The Nature of Change

You've already grasped that change is not just a passive component of our environment. It's active, alive, and fused into every element of our existence. Yet, despite its universality, we often find ourselves grappling to truly comprehend its nature and power. Let's dive deeper, shall we?

We can consider change as the heartbeat of the universe. Like nature, change comes in cycles—sometimes quickly, sometimes at a snail's pace, but we cannot deny that change is everywhere. Within the turn of the seasons, in the bloom of flowers, even within us as we grow and evolve. These rhythms of change are a testament to its resolute presence and influence.

Every era has had its defining moments of transformation. Ancient civilizations witnessed the dawn of agriculture, radically altering their lifestyles. The Industrial Revolution unveiled an era of machines, factories, and urbanization. Our present times are shaped by digital revolutions and technological innovations. In each phase, change sculpted the narrative.

Yet, as profound as these shifts are, they're merely the tip of the iceberg. Dive below the surface, and you'll find a deeper, more personal involvement with change—one that each individual experiences uniquely. Think back to your childhood dreams, aspirations, and beliefs. Now, compare them with your present convictions. Over time, our perspectives evolve, often so subtly that we hardly notice the transformation. These are our internal currents of change, guided by personal experiences, reflections, and growth. Larger societal, technological, and environmental trends also influence our collective experiences. When we talk about external triggers of change, we speak of events like economic shifts, groundbreaking innovations, or even global challenges such as pandemics. These forces, often beyond our direct control, push us to reevaluate, adapt, and evolve.

What we need to understand is that change itself is neutral. It doesn't carry a predetermined agenda nor play favorites. It presents a spectrum of possibilities waiting to be molded by our perceptions, reactions, and choices. This neutrality is what gives change its dynamic nature. When we perceive change as a threat, our reactions are driven by fear, leading to resistance or even paralysis. On the other hand, when we embrace change as an opportunity, our responses are motivated by curiosity, optimism, and a forward-looking mindset. The essence of 'The Power of Change' lies in learning to navigate the currents proactively, instead of just being carried away by them.

We *do* have the power to shape the outcome of change. It's a revelatory realization. The tools we employ—our mindset, resilience, strategies, and adaptability—influence the course of this transformation. The more skilled we become at directing the energies of change, the better we can form its outcomes to our advantage.

Every individual and organization has their unique "Change Story." Some stories are about leveraging change to reach new goals and aspirations. Others might be tales of resilience, learning from challenges, and emerging stronger. By internalizing the lessons from these stories and understanding the underlying currents, we can look to the future with greater insight and confidence.

The Power of Change implores us to change our perspective about change itself. We can cease to see change as a negative force, instead using its energy to push us forward. This reframing is essential because, as history and personal experiences show, those who understand and master the art of change become the torchbearers of progress.

With this understanding, every challenge becomes an opportunity, every setback a lesson, and every victory a stepping stone. This agile approach equips us to capture the power of change, ensuring that we're not just adapting reactively but leading proactively.

As we progress, keep in mind that change isn't just a series of events in the background; it's the driving force catapulting our narrative ahead. It connects our past experiences with our future goals. Understanding this gives us the power to take control, make wise decisions, and build a path to a resilient and hopeful future.

To truly understand the nature of change is to unlock the secrets of growth, progress, and evolution. By the end of our journey together, you'll be more than just coping with change – you'll be confidently and clearly making your own decisions. Welcome to *'The Power of Change.'* This experience is as educational as it is exciting. Let's build our changing futures together, learning step by step.

The Impact of Change on Individuals and Organizations

As we explore change on a deeper level, we begin to see patterns and recognize that there are multifaceted impacts of change, especially when we view it through two crucial lenses: the individual and the organizational.

The Personal Sphere: As we examine the individual, and you'll find change leaves permanent marks. Each one of us, with our unique emotional landscapes, aspirations, and experiences, becomes the stage where the drama of change unfolds.

Change can evoke profound emotional and cognitive responses, which in turn influence our worldview, actions, and decisions. Sometimes, change can be a revelatory journey. For instance, picture relocating to a place with an entirely different culture; such an alteration can lead in fresh perspectives and deeper global insights. However, the other side of the coin reveals change as a forerunner of anxiety and apprehension.

Think about crucial life moments - a career pivot or the peak of a significant relationship. These crossroads can shake our core, inducing self-doubt and sparking existential questions. Yet, amidst the turbulence lies a silver lining.

These very challenges, these moments of disruption, are often the catalysts for profound personal growth. They prompt us to venture beyond our comfort bubbles, to discover newfound resilience or skills. But for this metamorphosis to unfold, we must wear the lens of opportunity when gazing at change, not the spectacles of fear. Such a mindset transforms the labyrinth of change into a path of empowerment.

The Organizational Landscape: Beyond the personal sphere, change affects various entities, including businesses, startups, nonprofits, and governmental bodies. These entities operate in ever-evolving environments shaped by factors like technological advancements, societal shifts, regulatory changes, and market dynamics. These elements continually reshape the landscape of business. Adaptive, forward-thinking organizations can thrive by seizing opportunities brought by change, like technological advancements or shifting consumer preferences.

However, resistance to change, often driven by fear or attachment to the familiar, can hinder progress and innovation. Effective change management involves clear communication, empathetic leadership, inclusivity, and a commitment to learning. It's about valuing the human element within organizations. In the upcoming chapters, we'll explore the impacts of change and strategies not just to cope but to thrive. We'll demystify methods for embracing change, reducing resistance, and using it as a catalyst for growth. Understanding change's profound influence on both personal and collective narratives allows us to actively participate in shaping our destinies. Embracing change becomes a path of personal and collective evolution.

A Real-World Exploration: To fully capture the nature of change and its extensive consequences, it's most effective to base our conversation on actual situations. A prime example is a brand that, at its peak, defined mobile communication but later encountered the turbulent waves of change. Nokia, once the epitome of mobile phones, experienced and navigated major upheavals in the tech sector. Examining this case study reveals the effects of change on a business and offers important lessons in resilience, innovation, and strategic change. Let's explore the story of Nokia.

Case Study: The Digital Transformation of Nokia

Background: In the 1990s and early 2000s, if you lived in Europe (and indeed many other parts of the world), there was a high likelihood that your first mobile phone was a Nokia. The Finnish company dominated the mobile phone industry globally, known for its durable and reliable phones and, of course, the iconic game Snake.

The Advent of Smartphones: With the launch of Apple's iPhone in 2007 and the subsequent rise of Android devices, the mobile industry witnessed a significant shift toward smartphones. Touchscreens, app ecosystems, and mobile internet became the new norm. These devices weren't just phones—they were pocket-sized computers.

Nokia's Reaction: Nokia encountered formidable challenges as its once-dominant Symbian operating system became obsolete. The need to make critical decisions regarding a new operating system introduced a cloud of uncertainty that loomed over employees and their professional trajectories, raising questions about the future of their careers within the company.

The Impact and Pivot: Nokia's inability to adapt quickly to the smartphone revolution led to significant market share losses. The European once-giant of the mobile world had to make tough choices, eventually leading to the sale of its Devices and Services division to Microsoft in 2014. However, this marked the beginning of a new chapter in Nokia's history. With a firm commitment to adaptability, Nokia redirected its focus towards network infrastructure, leading to the establishment of Nokia Networks. Additionally, they ventured into other technology domains, diversifying their portfolio and demonstrating their ability to evolve and thrive amidst industry transformations.

Conclusion: This case study on Nokia is a testament to the profound impacts change can have on both organizations and individuals. While their initial response to the smartphone era was fraught with challenges, their eventual pivot showcases the importance of adaptability and resilience. It's a lesson for all: While change is inevitable, with the proper perspective and strategic choices, reinvention is always possible. Europe's tech landscape is dotted with tales of evolution, and Nokia's story serves as a poignant chapter in that larger narrative.

Understanding the Psychology of Change and Our Response to It

Moving along with our exploration of change, we're now setting foot into an immensely intriguing topic: the mind itself. Here, we'll unravel the complicated psychological processes that color our perception and reactions to change, whether as singular beings or as collective entities within organizations.

The Mind's Response to Change

Our first pitstop in this exploration is acknowledging that change disrupts our routines, introducing the unknown into our familiar lives. It stirs a range of emotions and thoughts, colored by our beliefs, past experiences, and dreams. These individual strands of our beliefs, values, and experiences greatly influence how we perceive and react to change. Previous rendezvous with change—the highs and lows—greatly affect our stance towards impending changes.

The Thinking Behind Change

Change pushes us to re-evaluate our actions, emotions, and thoughts. For example, adapting to a new role at work prompts us to learn new skills and adjust our habits. Similarly, societal changes like technological advancements lead us to revise our behaviors and ideologies to keep pace with the evolving landscape.

The Emotional Impact of Change

You cannot experience change without experiencing depth of emotion. Our feelings lend depth, nuance, and intensity to our experiences with change. They range from the exhilaration of new adventures to the anxiety of the unfamiliar. Making your way through emotional complexity requires emotional intelligence— the ability to constructively perceive, comprehend, and manage our feelings and those of others.

Intersecting Change and Self-Image

Our self-concept influences how we perceive change. Changes aligned with our self-image are accepted more readily, while those conflicting with it often face resistance. For instance, someone viewing themselves as an adventurer might eagerly seize the opportunity to study abroad, whereas someone more reserved might hesitate to take on roles requiring increased public interactions, as it may contradict their self-image.

Change's Echo in Organizations

Organizations also react to change based on their identity and norms. They embrace changes that align with their core beliefs, while those perceived as disruptive may encounter resistance. Harnessing this psychological insight can revolutionize how change is managed in organizations, emphasizing compassion, inclusivity, and transparent communication to validate emotions and viewpoints. In the upcoming sections, we will thoroughly examine these psychological complexities, illuminating the emotional and cognitive processes at play in adaptability. We will investigate how self-perceptions influence our reactions to change and how this understanding can promote smoother transitions at both personal and organizational levels. As we explore the mind's response to change, remember that understanding our internal reactions is crucial for harnessing the advantages of change and turning it from a formidable challenge into a catalyst for growth and progress.

The Unpredictable Rewards of Change

Before diving deep into the oft-confusing dynamics of change, let's pause for a moment and consider a real-world example that embodies the unpredictable rewards change can bring.

Steve Jobs, the iconic co-founder of Apple, often highlighted the non-linear path of his journey. In a memorable speech at Stanford University, he reflected on a seemingly inconsequential decision: attending a calligraphy class after dropping out of Reed College. This decision, trivial as it might have seemed, later became instrumental in shaping the distinctive look of the Macintosh computer. Drawing from his experience with beautiful lettering and typography, Jobs integrated what he learned into the design of the Mac, giving it an aesthetic edge over its competitors. "You can't connect the dots looking forward; you can only connect them looking backward," he remarked. This illustrates how change, even when its immediate benefits aren't clear, can set the stage for unexpected rewards down the line.

With this enlightening anecdote in mind, let's dive into the multifaceted nature of change...

The Contradictions of Change: Challenges and Opportunities

As we dig deeper into the nature of change, we encounter an interesting riddle: Change is both a challenge and a chance, a mystery littered with pitfalls and possibilities. This fascinating duality makes change not just a complex phenomenon but a compelling narrative of our lives and businesses. We'll unpack this duality, spotlighting the hurdles and highlights that punctuate our encounters with change.

The Rough Roads of Change

Look, it's no earth-shattering revelation that change brings its share of headaches and heartaches. Whether it's fear, stress, or downright resistance, change often gets greeted like an uninvited guest. Rooted deep in our psychology and even our evolutionary backstory, these knee-jerk reactions are often a tribute to our human wiring.

Why do we get so anxious? Well, change flings us into a jungle of unknowns and what-ifs. We humans are creatures of habit who love the comfort of the known landscape. An upheaval like an organizational shake-up sends us scrambling for answers. What will my next job entail? Should I update my skills? These are the kinds of uncertainties that often become sources of stress we struggle with.

It's not only about handling emotions; there's a practical side too. This involves mastering new methods, letting go of obsolete practices, and reorienting your mindset. In a business environment, this means dealing with operational challenges, juggling resources, and undertaking major strategic revisions.

The Silver Linings in Change

Let's look at it differently. Change isn't solely a source of challenges; it's also a treasure trove of opportunities. Growth, innovation, and progress are all closely tied to change. It acts as the catalyst that ignites new possibilities, pushing us to stretch, adapt, and grow.

Look at it from a business perspective, and you'll notice that change can fuel creativity and resilience. Organizations viewing change as a springboard, rather than a setback, typically excel in adapting. Consider the onset of the digital era; while it presented unexpected challenges, it also became a fertile ground for businesses willing to embrace adaptation and innovation. Change acts like a mirror, reflecting untapped potentials and unseen resilience. In wading through the turmoil that chance can bring, we often uncover latent facets of ourselves.

Making Sense of the Contradiction

Cracking the paradox of change—where the challenge meets the promise—means mastering the art of balance. We need to acknowledge the bumps without losing sight of the outlook. Resilience, a dash of daring, and a thirst for learning become your compass in this terrain of change. In the corridors of business, it's crucial to foster a culture where the pressures of change are openly discussed and addressed. Conversely, to fully capitalize on the benefits of change, we require a strategy that embraces a shift towards positivity, maintains an adaptable mindset, and concentrates intently on possibilities.

As we dive into the following chapters, we will continue this discussion—exploring the psychology of resilience and identifying strategies that enable us not only to survive but also to flourish in our constantly changing personal and professional environments.

In working through these complexities, let's remember that change is less a destination and more a dynamic journey. A rollercoaster ride of highs and lows, of trials and triumphs. And it's precisely this meandering path that enriches our growth, painting our canvas in hues of resilience, adaptability, and perpetual evolution.

Now that we've discussed how to recognize and understand the contradictions of change, I want you to take a moment for reflection. Reflecting on our personal experiences with change can provide rich insights, helping us to understand our reactions, identify patterns, and explore potential areas for growth.

Exercise

As we've moved through the kaleidoscope of emotions, identities, and cognitive processes surrounding change, it's time to turn the lens inward. Before we proceed, let's take a moment to embark on a personal journey. Using our own experiences and reflections can greatly deepen our comprehension.

Let's briefly shift our focus and engage fully in the activity: Reflecting on Personal Experiences with Change. This will serve as a connector between abstract concepts and our individual realities, providing an opportunity to deeply connect with all that we've explored. So go ahead, delve into your personal interactions with change and let your distinct experiences emerge. Before we go any farther, let's anchor ourselves with an exercise, breaking it down step by step:

Step 1: Recall a Pivotal Moment
Think back in time to a pivotal moment of change in your life. Perhaps it was a career leap, a geographical shift like relocating to a different place, or an inner metamorphosis. Let yourself soak in the memories, revisiting the essence of that phase.

Step 2: Dive into Your First Responses
Bring into focus your initial emotional and mental reactions to this shift. Did you greet it with enthusiasm, apprehension, resistance, or maybe a cocktail of emotions? Remember, this isn't about judging your reactions but gaining clarity on your personal experience with change.

Step 3: Unearth the Hurdles and Breakthroughs
Let's unearth a bit more. What were the challenges that this shift brought forth? The aspects you battled with? At the same time, highlight the opportunities that emerged due to this change. How did this transformation lead to new insights, knowledge, or experiences?

Step 4: Celebrate your Evolution
Look back and recognize the progress you made as a result of this change. Maybe you sharpened some skills, stumbled upon latent talents, or saw the world through a renewed lens. Each detail of your development, however small, is evidence of your continuously growing spirit.

Step 5: Harvesting Wisdom for What Lies Ahead
Lastly, extract valuable lessons from this reflection to navigate future changes. Think about the strategies that worked for you. Are there patterns in your experiences you'd want to adjust? Consider your key learnings - what you'd modify and what you'd hold dear. Returning to this exercise isn't a singular event; it's an ongoing

practice of self-examination. It's meant to be a resource for every new phase of change life brings your way. Approach this reflective process with compassion, an open mind, and eagerness for the insights you'll discover.

As we conclude this section and before you jump into applying this knowledge, let's pause briefly. Let's consolidate what we've covered into a few concise, impactful takeaways.

Key Takeaways

- Change? It's the unstoppable rhythm of life. It's not just something that happens to us; it's always around us, constantly moving and reshaping our lives.
- Forget about viewing change as just a wrinkle in our plans. Change is the driving force behind the growth, even when we least expect it.
- Change is predictable in its unpredictability. It can move at varying speeds, and rarely in as straight line.
- It's our mindset, our deeply-held beliefs, that color our glasses, influencing how we see and interact with change.
- Mastering the rhythm of change better prepares us to flow with life's transitions, rather than being hindered by them.
- Change isn't just a concept. It leaves footprints everywhere, sparking innovation and pushing growth but sometimes dropping challenges on our doorstep.
- Let's face it; accepting change can be difficult. Whether as individuals or businesses, we often resist due to fear or the comforting appeal of 'how things used to be.' Identifying and overcoming this resistance is key to managing change effectively.

- Here's the fun part of change: it's a two-faced coin. One side presents daunting challenges, but on the flip side, it reveals a wealth of opportunities and hidden gems ready to be uncovered.
- Reflecting on your own history of change isn't merely a trip down memory lane. It's a valuable guide, helping you comprehend your interaction with change and equipping you for future challenges.

Remember, comprehending change isn't about getting to an endpoint. It's about appreciating the journey of exploration, adaptation, and growth. Hold onto these insights as you navigate the constantly evolving paths of life and career.

CHAPTER 2

The Power of Change

D ive into "The Power of Change" and immerse yourself in the transformative energy of life's most constant element. In this chapter, we uncover the multifaceted nature of change. It is not merely a disturbance in our life's rhythm; it's a potent force that, when embraced, can act as a significant catalyst for growth and evolution. Hidden within its complexities are opportunities, sometimes subtle and at times glaring, waiting to be unearthed. Change, even when unexpected, can shape our story in many enriching ways.

But what about those moments when change isn't a gentle bump but a forceful push? Such compelled transitions can induce the most unlikely and often unexpected metamorphosis. But central to our journey is the realization that our perception of change, our very mindset, can make all the difference. Do we resist, or do we recalibrate and seize its power? Within this chapter, you'll find a renewed perspective on change, one that helps you not fear change but embrace it.

Prepare to redefine your relationship with change, transforming it from an adversary into one of your most empowering allies.

Embracing Change as a Catalyst for Growth

Change is a fundamental constant of our existence. It is as inevitable as the rising and setting of the sun. Yet, change isn't something we should fear or resist. Instead, we must recognize it as a potent catalyst for growth.

In our personal lives, change often steers in new experiences, opportunities, and perspectives that allow us to broaden our horizons and deepen our understanding of the world and ourselves. The journey from adolescence to adulthood, the transition from school to college, and then onto our professional lives are all significant milestones marked by change. These transitions can be challenging as they push us out of our comfort zones and demand us to adapt. But they also offer rich opportunities for self-discovery and personal development.

On an organizational level, change can be a powerful driver for innovation, competitiveness, and success. In the world of business, stagnation is a recipe for decline. To thrive and grow, organizations must continually evolve and adapt to their changing environment – be it shifts in consumer demands, technological advancements, or changes in regulations and policies.

Companies that embrace change tend to foster a culture of creativity and innovation. They are more agile and resilient, able to pivot their strategies and operations to capitalize on new opportunities and navigate challenges. They also attract and retain top talents who value dynamic work environments and opportunities for professional growth and advancement.

However, leveraging change as a catalyst for growth requires more than just passively accepting or enduring it. It demands a proactive approach characterized by open-mindedness, flexibility, resilience, and a willingness to take calculated risks. It involves viewing change not as a threat to our established ways of life or operations but as a vehicle for improvement and advancement.

To rein in the power of change for personal growth, we must cultivate an open and adaptive mindset. We need to be willing to let go of old habits and beliefs that no longer serve us and be ready to learn, grow, and evolve. We need to see the challenges that come with change as opportunities to test our skills, build resilience, and learn valuable life lessons.

For organizations, embracing change involves fostering a culture that values innovation, encourages learning, and rewards risk-taking. It requires strong leadership to guide the organization through periods of change and uncertainty and effective communication to keep everyone informed and engaged. It also necessitates developing organizational structures and processes that are flexible and adaptable, capable of supporting change rather than hindering it.

We have to remember that embracing change is about more than just surviving in a rapidly changing world. It's about seizing the opportunities presented by change to learn, grow, and thrive. It's about transforming the fear of the unknown into excitement for what could be. It's about recognizing that every end is a new beginning, and every challenge is an opportunity in disguise. As we move through the following sections, we'll dig deeper into corralling the power of change to unleash hidden personal and professional potential, including strategies and techniques for embracing change, overcoming resistance, and turning the inevitable into the inspirational.

Discovering Opportunities in the Midst of Change

Change, though often seen as an inevitable part of life, carries within it a multitude of opportunities waiting to be uncovered. These opportunities can guide us toward personal and professional growth, innovation, and advancement. Often, we perceive change as something that disrupts our stability, casting us into uncertainty and discomfort. However, a different perspective can help us identify the chances for improvement, development, and innovation that change brings. Seeing change through the lens of opportunity requires an adjustment of our mindset, an openness to explore the unfamiliar, and a willingness to work through the inevitable challenges that accompany these periods of transition. In our personal lives, change can lead to self-discovery, unveiling hidden facets of our character and potential. Consider the process of moving to a new city or country. While the transition may be daunting, it also presents a chance for personal growth. We get to experience new cultures, meet diverse individuals, and learn to make your way in an unfamiliar environment, all of which broaden our horizons and enrich our understanding of the world. Similarly, experiencing a career change, whether voluntary or forced, opens the door to developing new skills, expanding our networks, and discovering untapped potential. While the initial shock or uncertainty can be unsettling, the potential for growth that lies within these changes is vast.

For organizations, change provides a platform for innovation and progress. While challenging, changes in market trends, customer preferences, or technological advancements also open up new avenues for growth and competitiveness. By staying agile and responsive to these shifts, businesses can identify emerging markets, develop novel products and services, and establish a strong foothold in their industry.

Take the case of industries that have faced disruption due to technological advancements. Organizations that viewed these changes as opportunities to innovate have reaped substantial rewards. The evolution of digital streaming platforms is an excellent example of this. Companies like Netflix and Spotify saw the change in consumer behavior towards online streaming and seized the opportunity to provide a novel and popular service.

Unearthing these hidden opportunities amidst change, however, requires certain key strategies. It involves maintaining an open and adaptive mindset that encourages exploration and experimentation. It calls for the ability to adapt quickly, turning on a dime when necessary. It demands courage to face the discomfort that often accompanies the unknown. Most importantly, it needs an unwavering belief in our potential and capacities. Both as individuals and organizations, we must trust in our ability to learn, grow, and adapt, regardless of the circumstances. This belief acts as the compass guiding us through the complexities of change, leading us towards the opportunities lying hidden amidst the chaos.

Let's take a closer look at the transformative effects of forced change, exploring how such circumstances can be leveraged for growth and progress. We'll also discuss the importance of cultivating an embracing change mindset, which is crucial in shifting our perspectives towards change and unearthing the hidden treasures it holds.

Remember, change, in its various forms and intensities, is a constant companion on our life journey. But with the right mindset and strategies, we can transform it into a powerful tool, leading us towards unseen opportunities and uncharted territories of growth.

The Transformative Effects of Forced Change

Though often met with resistance and apprehension, forced change possesses a transformative power that can dramatically alter our personal lives and professional landscapes. These are changes thrust upon us, either by unexpected circumstances, significant events, or external shifts beyond our control. They might appear in the form of job loss, sudden relocations, policy changes, technological disruptions, or global events, such as the COVID-19 pandemic.

Indeed, forced change can initially seem like a hurdle, uprooting our comfort and demanding rapid adaptation. It might evoke feelings of fear, insecurity, and uncertainty. We might yearn for the stability of the past and resist the new reality, struggling to comprehend its implications. However, within this whirlwind of forced change lies an inherent potential for profound transformation and growth.

It may help to think of forced change as a metamorphosis; while it can be painful, something beautiful emerges. Forced change can be painful—remember, the caterpillar inside the chrysalis is broken down to its very cellular level before being put back together as a butterfly. This is the essence of forced change. Though it may be challenging and cause hurt, forced change serves as a catalyst for transformation. It pushes us to survive, evolve, innovate, and thrive.

On a personal level, forced changes often act as a wake-up call, making us reevaluate our values, priorities, and paths. Changes gracelessly shove us out of complacency, compelling us to learn, grow, and adapt in ways we might never have considered. We might discover strengths we didn't know we possessed, interests we hadn't explored, or opportunities we hadn't seen before. In essence, forced changes can act as powerful turning points, steering us towards new horizons of personal development and fulfillment.

In the professional realm, forced changes can drive innovation and progress, even amidst uncertainty. Businesses that view these changes as opportunities to adapt and evolve are the ones that survive and thrive. The rise of remote work due to the pandemic is a prime example. Organizations were compelled to adjust their operating models almost overnight. Those who embraced this change have discovered numerous benefits, such as reduced overhead costs, increased employee satisfaction, and access to a broader talent pool.

However, benefitting from the transformative nature of forced change requires specific strategies. It calls for resilience – the capacity to bounce back from adversity and emerge stronger. It demands flexibility – the ability to adapt to new circumstances. It needs a positive outlook – viewing challenges as opportunities for growth rather than overwhelming obstacles. Reaping the benefits of forced change also requires patience and compassion towards ourselves and others. Forced change can be a tumultuous process, laden with fear and uncertainty. Therefore, it's crucial to approach it with empathy, understanding that it's okay to feel unsettled and to take time to adjust.

Though disruptive and challenging, forced changes hold a transformative potential that can catalyze personal growth and organizational innovation. The key lies in shifting our perspective, from viewing these changes as threats to perceiving them as opportunities for evolution. Remember, in the midst of every crisis lies great opportunity.

It becomes essential to frame our experiences with forced change around tangible examples of success. History is full of stories of enterprises and individuals who've tangled with change, for better or worse. One such story is that of Sony. This global powerhouse faced its own turbulent period of transformation, where it not only met change eye-to-eye but also turned it into a shining example of innovation and resurgence.

Case Study: The Transformation of Sony - Embracing Change After a Crisis

Background: Founded in 1946 in Tokyo, Japan, Sony emerged as a leader in the electronics industry, known for innovations like the Walkman, PlayStation, and Trinitron TVs. However, by the late 2000s, Sony found itself lagging behind competitors, particularly in the television segment, due to the rapid rise of South Korean companies like Samsung and LG.

The Challenge: The global financial crisis of 2008, combined with stiff competition from other Asian electronics giants, put significant financial strain on Sony. Their traditional areas of strength, such as televisions and portable music players, were no longer as profitable or in demand.

Forced Change and Transformation: Sony tackled this forced change by making the most out of three opportunities to regain their market share.

1. Shift to New Business Areas: Sony began investing more heavily in areas like gaming (PlayStation), movies (Sony Pictures), and financial services (Sony Financial). This diversification helped mitigate the losses from their electronics segment.

2. Organizational Restructuring: In 2012, Kazuo Hirai took over as CEO and initiated "One Sony," an aggressive restructuring strategy to streamline operations and foster inter-departmental collaboration.

3. Embracing New Technology and Innovation: Sony started focusing more on areas like sensors for cameras and smartphones, Virtual Reality (through PlayStation VR), and other emerging tech fields.

Outcome: Sony's willingness to change its business model, diversify its portfolio, and restructure internally allowed it to bounce back. By 2018, their stock prices reached a ten-year high, signaling a successful turnaround. Their transformation showcases how timely adaptation and a willingness to venture into new areas can lead to rejuvenation even after facing seemingly insurmountable challenges.

Reflections: When confronted with forced changes, companies often need to introspect and find new avenues of growth and revenue. Sony's journey illustrates how embracing change, diversifying risk, and fostering innovation can pave the way for resurgence. In an ever-evolving global market, clinging to past success isn't enough; continual reinvention is key.

While large corporations like Sony paint a broader picture of embracing change, it's sometimes the individual journeys, filled with grit and resilience, that deeply resonate with our personal experiences. Among these tales, the narrative of Jack Ma stands out—not just because of the colossal empire he built but also due to the myriad of challenges that he was able to transform into stepping stones. Let's examine Ma's story, drawing parallels and insights for our own paths of change and growth.

Case Study: Jack Ma - Embracing the Unknown

Background: Jack Ma, the iconic figure behind Alibaba Group, hails from Hangzhou, China. Today, he's a symbol of entrepreneurship and innovation, but his journey was anything but straightforward. From being a humble English teacher to helming one of the largest e-commerce platforms globally, Jack's life story offers profound insights into how forced change can shape destinies.

The Challenge: Jack faced numerous rejections throughout his early life. He failed his college entrance exam twice and was turned down for multiple jobs, even being rejected by KFC when it opened in his hometown. However, during a trip to the United States in the 1990s, he was introduced to the Internet, sensing its potential in China.

The Transformative Effects of Forced Change: Just like Sony was able to see beyond the turmoil of the moment, Jack Ma was also able to envision himself on the far side of change and find a way to traverse uncertainty and achieve success amidst the uncertainty of forced change.

1. Adapting to a New Vision: Recognizing the potential of the Internet for business, Jack launched his first venture, China Pages, creating websites for Chinese companies. Though it didn't succeed as planned, it planted the seed for what would come.

2. Overcoming Skepticism: Jack founded Alibaba in his apartment with a group of friends in 1999. The goal was clear: create a platform for small and medium-sized businesses to sell globally. Many were skeptical about e-commerce in China at the time, but Jack believed in the transformative power of the Internet.

3. Facing the Giants: As Alibaba grew, it faced stiff competition from global giants like eBay. Instead of backing down, Jack Ma used his local knowledge to adapt Alibaba's business model to better fit Chinese consumers, ultimately outpacing foreign competitors.

Outcome: Alibaba's meteoric rise changed the face of e-commerce and technology in China. It not only thrust Jack Ma into international fame but also showcased the power of vision, adaptability, and tenacity.

Reflections: Jack Ma's journey underscores the essence of embracing change. Even in the face of failures, setbacks, and massive competition, it's possible to carve out a transformative path. The key lies in adapting, learning from every experience, and having an unwavering belief in one's vision. In business and in life, it's not the challenges that define us but how we respond to them. Change, even when forced, can catalyze revolutionary ideas and unprecedented success.

Embracing Change Mindset to Shift Perspectives and Achieve Success

As we move further into our exploration of change, we begin to realize that our mindset, the mental attitudes and beliefs we hold, plays a significant role in how we navigate change. Our mindset determines how we perceive change, and thus, it influences how we react and adapt to it. Embracing a change mindset means adopting a perspective where change isn't seen as a threat or a disruption but as an opportunity for growth and innovation. The concept of a change mindset is not just about accepting change; it's about seeking it out, craving it even. It's about understanding that the status quo can be challenged and that there's always room for improvement. It's about realizing that it's not just about survival amidst change but about thriving, about leveraging the opportunities that change presents.

This Change Mindset, however, is multifaceted.

One key aspect of the Change Mindset is resilience - the capacity to bounce back from challenges and adversities. Change, especially when it is unexpected or significant, can often be stressful. However, if we cultivate resilience, we can work through these changes with strength and courage. We can learn from our experiences, grow from our mistakes, and continually evolve towards better versions of ourselves.

Another critical element of the Change Mindset is positivity. A positive attitude helps us see the opportunities embedded in change rather than focusing on the difficulties or losses. It allows us to focus on our strengths, celebrate our victories, and maintain a sense of optimism, even in challenging times.

The Change Mindset also goes beyond resilience and positivity, **invoking a sense of curiosity** and a desire for continuous learning. In a rapidly changing world, learning, unlearning, and relearning is crucial. It enables us to stay relevant, adapt to new situations, and seize the opportunities that come our way.

Finally, the Change Mindset entails embracing uncertainty. The future is inherently uncertain, and no amount of planning can accurately predict it. Instead of fearing this uncertainty, we can choose to embrace it. We can see it as a space of endless possibilities where we can shape our destinies and create our futures. We all need to keep in mind that cultivating a change mindset is not a simple switch to be flipped. It involves a continuous journey of self-awareness, learning, and adaptation. It requires a willingness to step out of our comfort zones, confront our fears and uncertainties, and venture into the unknown. It necessitates acknowledging our resistance to change, understanding its roots, and consciously working towards overcoming it. On an individual level, embracing a change mindset can lead to personal growth and transformation. In organizations, a change mindset can become a strategic asset. Creating a culture that embraces a change mindset involves nurturing openness, fostering learning and innovation, and celebrating failures as opportunities for learning. Strong leadership that supports employees through the transition is pivotal. As we close this chapter, reflect on your mindset towards change. How do you typically respond to change? What fears and resistance do you have, and how can you work towards overcoming them? What steps can you take to cultivate a change mindset, both in your personal life and in your organization? Remember, the power to thrive amidst change lies within you. All it takes is a shift in perspective.

Exercise: Identifying Personal Goals for Embracing Change

Begin by finding a quiet space where you can be uninterrupted for a few moments. Have a pen and a notebook at hand, or perhaps your preferred digital note-taking device.

1. Start with Reflection: Look back at your life and identify instances where you've successfully adapted to change. How did it make you feel? What did you learn from these experiences? Write these down.

2. Analyze Your Attitude: Take a moment to reflect on your current mindset towards change. Are you usually open and flexible, or do you resist change? It's important to be honest with yourself during this step. Remember, acknowledging a need for improvement is the first step towards growth.

3. Define Your Goals: Now, let's focus on the future. Write down what you would like to achieve in terms of embracing change. Be specific. Your goals might range from developing a more positive attitude towards change, improving your adaptability skills, or learning new strategies to manage stress during times of change.

4. Action Steps: Break down each of your goals into small, manageable steps. What are the actions you need to take to achieve these goals? They could be daily habits, like practicing mindfulness, or larger efforts, such as taking a course on change management.

5. Set a Timeline: Assign a timeline to each of your action steps. This provides you with a roadmap and keeps you accountable.

6. Regular Reviews: Lastly, schedule regular intervals to review your progress. This could be once a month or once a quarter, depending on your preference. Reflect on your journey, celebrate your victories, and adjust your actions as necessary.

Remember, embracing change is a journey, not a destination. Be patient with yourself, and remember to appreciate the process. With each small victory, you're becoming more skilled at navigating and utilizing change for your personal and professional growth. It's about continuously learning, adapting, and growing. Embrace change, embrace growth!

Key Takeaways

- Change is a powerful, unending force that, when embraced, can be a catalyst for significant growth and progress.
- Opportunities often lie hidden amidst change. By adopting an open and exploratory attitude, we can discover and leverage these opportunities for innovation and transformation.
- Forced change, while potentially disruptive, can have transformative effects. It often demands that we go out of our comfort zones, triggering growth and breakthroughs we might not have achieved otherwise.
- Cultivating an 'Embracing Change Mindset' is crucial for the successful management of change. This mindset is characterized by flexibility, adaptability, resilience, positivity, a desire for continuous learning, and a willingness to embrace uncertainty.
- Resilience is a vital aspect of the Change Mindset. It enables us to bounce back from challenges, learn from our experiences, and continually evolve.
- A positive attitude allows us to focus on opportunities and strengths rather than difficulties, fostering a sense of optimism even in challenging times.
- Fostering curiosity and continuous learning is critical in a rapidly changing world. It equips us with the ability to adapt, stay relevant, and seize new opportunities.
- Embracing uncertainty, rather than fearing it, allows us to perceive it as a space of endless possibilities, where we can shape our destinies and create our futures.
- By adopting a Change Mindset, we become proactive rather than reactive, leveraging the power of change to drive personal and professional growth, fulfillment, and success.

CHAPTER 3

Change and Time—Moore's Law and Beyond

In this chapter, we will explore the fascinating connection between change and time, particularly through the lens of
Moore's Law. We'll unpack how this law—originally conceived
to describe the exponential growth in computing power—can be
applied as a metaphor for the rapid pace of change in our world
today. We'll closely examine the implications of living in a time
when change is inevitable and accelerates with each passing moment.

We'll examine how technology's rapid advancement influences
our perception of time and change and how it significantly impacts various sectors, transforming economies, reshaping societies, and altering individual lives. We'll also take a look at the
strategies required to adapt efficiently in this era of rapid technological innovation and disruption.

The objective here is to cultivate an understanding and acceptance of our fast-paced world, learning to work through the
challenges and opportunities it presents, thereby positioning ourselves for success in the continuously evolving landscape of tomorrow.

The Accelerating Pace of Change: Understanding Moore's Law

Moore's Law, named after Gordon Moore, co-founder of Fairchild Semiconductor and Intel, is a concept that laid the foundation for the incredible journey of technological progress over the last half-century. In 1965, Moore initially observed that the number of transistors on a microchip doubled approximately every two years while the cost of those computers was halved. In simple terms, this means that computing power would dramatically increase over time, providing us with stronger, faster, and more efficient devices at a lower cost.

Moore's Law is fascinating because of both its incredibly accurate prediction and its broader metaphorical implications. While it began as an observation about semiconductor manufacturing, Moore's Law represents an expectation of rapid, continuous technological change and progress in our society. We see this exponential growth all around us, not just in terms of technology but in almost every aspect of our lives. From the growth of the internet and smartphones to artificial intelligence and biotechnology, the acceleration is tangible. The last few decades have brought about changes that might have taken centuries to accomplish in the past.

However, this rapid pace of change is not without its challenges. It often outpaces our ability to understand and keep up with it, leaving us overwhelmed and disoriented. As we race ahead on the technology front, we also face the ethical, social, and emotional consequences of these advancements, raising important questions about data privacy, security, job displacement, and the digital divide.

Understanding and adapting to this accelerating pace of change require us to evolve our ways of thinking and acting.

We need to develop digital literacy, cultivate a mindset of lifelong learning, and remain agile in the face of change. We must be open to unlearning outdated information and learning new things, a crucial process in an era where new technologies can render previous knowledge obsolete in a matter of years, if not months.

It's important to note that while Moore's Law drives much of this acceleration, it's not an unbreakable law of nature. Physical and economic limits exist on how much we can keep shrinking transistors and doubling chip performance. However, as we hit these limits, new technologies and frameworks, such as quantum computing and artificial intelligence, emerge to take the baton of rapid progress forward.

We need to understand that Moore's Law isn't just about comprehending the course of technological progress; it's about grasping the nature of change in our modern world and learning to manage it effectively. We are all working toward the same goal—to understand how things change, why things change, and the best way to adapt.

The Impact of Technological Advancements on Change Dynamics

As we continue our exploration of change, we can't overlook the profound influence of technological advancements on change dynamics. We find ourselves in an era of technological marvels, from the Internet of Things (IoT), AI, robotics, and quantum computing to biotechnology, where each development sets in motion a domino effect of changes that fundamentally transform our lives.

The reach of technology is vast and all-encompassing. It's not confined to any single area of life; these technological advancements impact us at varying levels in every facet of our existence. At an individual level, technology has radically altered our daily lives. Smartphones keep us connected to the world, wearable devices monitor our health, apps help manage our finances, and AI-powered assistants simplify tasks. It's about how we work, learn, communicate, and even how we perceive ourselves. Each new technology shifts our behavior, mindset, and lifestyle.

We do need to acknowledge that these changes aren't always linear or universally beneficial. The digital divide between those with access to technology and those without has widened. Not everyone has the digital literacy required to negotiate the complex modern landscape, which raises questions about inclusivity, fairness, and justice.

At an organizational level, technological advancements are reshaping businesses and industries at a breakneck pace. Digital transformation has become the mantra for survival and success. Companies leverage big data, AI, cloud computing, and other technologies to streamline operations, enhance customer experiences, and drive innovation. But this shift requires agility, a willingness to take risks, and a culture that promotes continuous learning and adaptability. Again, challenges exist. Cybersecurity threats loom large, and ethical considerations around data privacy and AI bias are increasingly pressing. Additionally, the rapid pace of technological advancements often outpaces regulatory frameworks, creating a gap that can lead to misuse and unforeseen consequences.

On a societal level, technological advancements are redefining our social fabric. How we interact, form communities, share information, and engage in civic discourse has been transformed. Social media platforms and the digital public square they create have led in a new era of social dynamics—with all its opportunities for connection *and* all its challenges, such as fake news, online bullying, and echo chambers.

Finally, on a global level, technology is a powerful force that drives large-scale changes. It shapes geopolitics, global economy, environmental policy, and space exploration. From blockchain's potential to disrupt financial systems to AI's role in combating climate change to the possibilities of space technologies, we are witnessing a future once confined to science fiction becoming a reality.

We must remember that technology isn't merely a tool; it's an agent of change – powerful, transformative, and at times, disruptive. Understanding the impact of technological advancements on change dynamics isn't an option but a necessity for individuals, organizations, and societies aiming to survive, grow, and thrive in the digital future.

Embracing Disruption and Innovation in the Digital Age

A critical factor that defines our journey, digital or otherwise, is how effectively we adapt. This technological age, marked by continuous disruption and incessant innovation, presents both challenges and opportunities. Let's explore the art of embracing disruption and the power of innovation as crucial tools in mastering the potential of this dynamic landscape.

The digital age has turned the world into a colossal, interconnected ecosystem. This boundless connectivity, powered by digital technologies, has paved the way for revolutionary changes that
have disrupted our norms, paradigms, and traditional ways of living and working. But disruption isn't inherently negative. It's a
powerful force that breaks down old structures to make way for
new ones, propelling us towards progress.

Let's consider the business landscape. Today, startups disrupt established markets with innovative business models, products, and
services. Traditional brick-and-mortar businesses find themselves competing with digital-first enterprises that leverage technology to offer enhanced customer experiences, greater efficiency, and global reach. Though challenging for many established
players, this disruption also brings unprecedented opportunities
for innovation, growth, and differentiation.

Adapting to this disruptive landscape requires agility and a willingness to continuously explore, experiment, and learn. It requires us to be comfortable with uncertainty and to develop resilience in the face of fast-paced changes. It also calls for a radical
shift in mindset: viewing disruption not as a threat but as a catalyst for innovation and transformation.

It's important to realize that innovation isn't limited to creating
groundbreaking technologies or products. It's about finding new
ways to solve problems, to serve customers, and to deliver value.
It's about fostering a culture that encourages creative thinking,
embraces diversity, and learns from failures. At its core, innovation is a mindset, a way of seeing and responding to the world
around us. The key to adapting to the digital age is the ability to
learn, unlearn, and relearn. This iterative learning process is vital
to keep pace with the rapid technological advancements and

changing market dynamics. It's about continuously upgrading our skills, staying abreast of emerging trends, and being open to new ideas and perspectives.

How do we jump into the iterative learning cycle? It begins with cultivating digital literacy: understanding digital technologies, their applications, and their implications. It's about becoming a discerning digital consumer, aware of cybersecurity threats and mindful of digital ethics. It involves developing digital skills relevant to our work, interests, and lives.

Adapting to the digital age also involves cultivating an innovation mindset. This involves curiosity, asking questions, challenging the status quo, and experimenting with new ideas. It's about learning from failures, trying again, and evolving. An innovation mindset sees opportunities in challenges and treats problems as puzzles to be solved. Adapting to the digital age also means understanding our role in shaping the digital landscape. As users, consumers, creators, and citizens, we have a say in shaping our digital experiences, norms, and policies. Although the flux and flow of the digital age may seem overwhelming at times, it's crucial to remember that our choices, actions, and voices matter.

Balancing Time and Change: Strategies for Efficient Adaptation

In trying to understand the intersection of time and change, we often seek the most efficient path toward adaptation. The balance between time and change is a delicate equilibrium that we continually try to maintain. With the accelerating pace of change in a digital world, finding the right strategies to adapt effectively within the constraints of time becomes all the more crucial.

To begin understanding time and change, we have to acknowledge that time, a resource unlike any other, is a fixed constant in our lives. How we perceive and utilize time can significantly impact our journey towards embracing change. Understanding that change is a process and not a destination, we need to align our perceptions of time accordingly. We should work *with* time, not see time as an enemy working *against* us.

Adapting to change doesn't necessarily mean reacting hastily to every new trend or emerging technology. Instead, efficient adaptation involves a measured, thoughtful response. It requires us to assess the potential impact of the change, the resources at our disposal, and our readiness to adapt. Doing so allows us to prioritize our actions and use our time effectively.

The first strategy for efficient adaptation is mindfulness. Being mindful lets us recognize the ongoing changes within and around us. It brings our focus to the present moment, creating a space for understanding the implications of change and our response to it. Mindfulness brings clarity, reduces stress, and helps us make informed decisions, making the adaptation process smoother and more efficient. The second strategy revolves around continuous learning. With the ever-evolving technological landscape, we must commit to lifelong learning. But remember, learning should not be a race against time but an ongoing journey marked by curiosity and exploration. It's about finding the right pace for ourselves and focusing on building depth in our knowledge rather than trying to cover everything. This way, learning becomes an enjoyable process rather than a stressful chore. Thirdly, efficient adaptation is about resilience and flexibility. We must cultivate the ability to bounce back from setbacks and maintain our momentum in the face of adversity. Simultaneously, flexibility enables us to adjust our strategies when required, allowing us to manage change with more ease and less friction. The fourth strategy for efficient adaptation involves creating support systems. Relationships and connections can be a significant source of strength during times of change. Establishing strong networks of support, both personally and professionally, can provide the guidance, encouragement, and resources needed for effective adaptation. Lastly, embracing change involves adopting a growth mindset. This mindset regards challenges as opportunities for learning and growth rather than obstacles. It fosters a sense of optimism, opening our minds to new possibilities and encouraging us to step out of our comfort zones. Remember that in the face of constant change, our ability to adapt effectively becomes our greatest asset. After thoroughly unpacking the implications of Moore's Law and exploring how this exponential growth model has been the backbone of technological advancement *and* a model that we can use to map personal growth, it's time to shift our focus from theory to tangible execution. Let's look at this chapter's case study and take a trip into the fascinating world of semiconductor manufacturing with Taiwan Semiconductor Manufacturing Company, better known as TSMC. From pioneering the foundry model to pushing the boundaries of silicon innovation, TSMC is a benchmark of what embracing the speed of change can do. As we examine their journey, we'll discover not just a case study but a playbook on how organizations can manipulate the power of change, anticipate the future, and mold it in their favor. This particular case is incredible because of the sheer velocity of technological change.

Case Study: TSMC - Championing the Semiconductor Revolution

Backdrop: Hsinchu, Taiwan, 1987. The semiconductor landscape was dominated by integrated device manufacturers (IDMs) that designed, manufactured, and marketed their chips. The idea of "fabless" semiconductor companies was emerging, but there was a missing link: who would manufacture for them?

Enter TSMC: Morris Chang, with his vision for the semiconductor industry, founded Taiwan Semiconductor Manufacturing Company (TSMC). Recognizing the potential of Moore's Law and the ever-shrinking transistor size, he introduced a novel business model.

The Pure-Play Foundry Model:

1. Fabless Future: TSMC pioneered the dedicated semiconductor foundry business model. They focused solely on manufacturing, allowing design companies to remain "fabless", concentrating on chip design without the burden of managing expensive manufacturing (fabrication) plants.

2. Riding the Wave of Moore's Law: As transistors got smaller, chips became more powerful and efficient. TSMC invested heavily in R&D to ensure they were at the cutting edge of manufacturing technology, often leading the industry in transitioning to smaller transistor nodes.

3. Global Partnerships: Understanding the global nature of technological advancements, TSMC collaborated with tech giants, ensuring a steady demand for their manufacturing capabilities.

4. Flexible and Scalable: By focusing solely on manufacturing and regularly upgrading their processes, TSMC could flexibly cater to various client demands, from high-performance computing chips to power-efficient mobile processors.

Today's Landscape: TSMC's approach revolutionized the semiconductor industry. Their foundry model enabled a surge in semiconductor startups and innovations, which would have been impossible in the IDM-dominated era. Today, TSMC is the world's most valuable semiconductor company, playing a pivotal role in the tech industry.

Reflection: Morris Chang's vision and the subsequent rise of TSMC underscore the significance of foresight in the tech world. They didn't merely react to Moore's Law; they anchored their business strategy on it. In doing so, TSMC has facilitated countless technological advancements and remains a testament to the power of strategic adaptability amidst exponential technological growth.

In this case study of TSMC, there's a profound lesson on leveraging technological forecasts for survival and unparalleled growth and industry transformation. As we reflect on the seismic shifts stemming from TSMC's contributions to semiconductor innovation—a story that epitomizes the relentless march of Moore's Law—our minds may naturally gravitate towards the question: who takes these technological marvels and pushes them in ways that stretch our collective imagination?

The answer: *visionaries who embody the essence of "The Power of Change" with every fiber of their being.*

These individuals don't just adapt to change; they create, shape, and use it as a springboard for humanity's next giant leap. Let's consider someone who is practically a living embodiment of Moore's Law. A person who travels in the circles of multiple industries, morphing challenges into stepping stones towards a future so expansive that it literally aims for the stars.

Enter Elon Musk—entrepreneur, innovator, and a master of change: From SpaceX's aspirations of interplanetary living to Tesla's reinvention of sustainable transportation, Musk takes the exponential growth heralded by Moore's Law and applies it as a foundational philosophy across ventures. Ready to get your mind blown?

Let's explore how Musk's endeavors offer a panoramic view of embracing change in an era defined by the acceleration of progress.

Elon Musk and the Acceleration of Progress

Elon Musk, the maverick entrepreneur behind companies like Tesla, SpaceX, Neuralink, and The Boring Company, is a testament to the exponential growth mindset. His ventures into various industries—ranging from automotive to aerospace to neural technology—allude to a larger narrative: the idea that in an era of rapid technological change, boundless opportunities emerge for those willing to embrace them.

Here's a breakdown of Musk's ventures.

SpaceX: While Moore's Law speaks predominantly about doubling transistors on a chip, Musk's endeavors with SpaceX offer a broader interpretation. Here's a company that aims to reduce space travel costs and make life multi-planetary. This audacious goal, reminiscent of the big leaps expected from the implications of Moore's Law, shows that exponential thinking isn't restricted to semiconductors.

Tesla: With Tesla, Musk revolutionized the electric vehicle industry, setting it on an exponential growth path.

The evolution of Tesla's battery technology, production efficiency, and software integration is a real-world testament to the rapid pace of innovation driven by vision and purpose.

Neuralink: Pushing the boundaries even further, Neuralink dives deep into the merging of man and machine. This venture underscores the idea that the fusion of biology and technology is the next frontier, resonating with the underpinnings of Moore's Law – that as technology advances, previously unthinkable possibilities become realities.

Musk's work embodies the spirit of viewing change as not a linear progression but an exponential curve. By anticipating where technology can be, not just where it is, Musk showcases how visionaries can grapple with change, manage the challenges of time, and accelerate toward daring goals.

Exercise: Exploring the Role of Technology in Your Life

When it comes to technology, balance is key. Let's attempt to make sense of the role of technology in our lives. This exercise will help us assess how much technology influences our day-to-day activities and how we can use it more effectively to embrace change.

Step 1: Document your Daily Interactions with Technology

For one week, keep a journal of all your interactions with technology. From checking your phone in the morning to using the microwave, from your work-related activities on your laptop to winding down with Netflix in the evening - jot it all down. This exercise is not to judge or critique but to create awareness about our digital behavior.

Step 2: Analyze your Journal

After a week, take some time to go through your journal. Look for patterns. How much time are you spending on technology? What types of activities are you engaging in? Are these activities more of leisure or work? Is there a balance?

Step 3: Identify Areas for Improvement

Based on your analysis, identify areas where you might need to cut back or enhance your engagement with technology. Maybe you're spending too much time on social media, affecting your productivity. Or perhaps you're not leveraging technology enough for personal development, like online learning platforms.

Step 4: Set Goals

Now, set some goals for how you would like your engagement with technology to look. These goals should be specific, measurable, achievable, relevant, and time-bound (SMART). For instance, you could aim to reduce your daily social media use by 30 minutes for the next month.

Step 5: Implement and Reflect

These changes and continue documenting your interactions with technology. Reflect on how these changes are affecting other areas of your life. Remember, it's okay if you stumble. The idea is to keep learning, growing, and adapting. Because change is inevitable, technology is a powerful tool that, when used effectively, can aid us in embracing that change. This exercise is a step toward understanding and using that power to our advantage. Remember, it's not about completely eliminating technology from our lives but finding a balance where we can enjoy the benefits without being overwhelmed. It's about ensuring technology serves us, not the other way around.

Exercise: Mastering Your Time

Understanding how we manage our time is crucial to efficiently adapting to change. This exercise is all about taking control of your time and using it as a powerful tool for adaptation and growth.

This exercise will help you uncover and understand your personal relationship with time and change.

Step 1: Time Audit
For one week, keep a detailed log of your activities and the time spent on each. It's essential to include everything from your daily commute to the time spent scrolling through social media to those vital hours spent on work or personal development. This isn't about judgment but about getting a clear picture of your current time allocation.

Step 2: Review and Reflect
At the end of the week, look honestly at your log. Where is the bulk of your time going? Are there any surprises? Are you dedicating enough time to your priorities or getting caught up in less important tasks?

Step 3: Prioritize
Identify the activities that align with your goals and contribute to your growth. These should be your high-priority tasks. At the same time, recognize the low-value tasks or possible time-wasters.

Step 4: Set Time Management Goals
Now that you've got a sense of your time usage and priorities, set specific, achievable goals to shift time from low-value activities to

high-value ones. Remember, the aim is not to fill every moment with productivity but to ensure your time aligns with your values and priorities.

Step 5: Implement and Adjust

Start making changes based on your set goals. If you've decided to cut down on social media, use app limit features. If you want to spend more time on personal development, schedule it in. Review your progress regularly and make adjustments as necessary.

Mastering your time is a continuous process of reflection, adjustment, and improvement. It's not about perfection but about making conscious decisions that lead you closer to your goals, one day at a time. Remember that time is our partner, not our enemy, and learning to work with it is a skill worth practicing.

Let's continue taking steps towards a better understanding and use of our time, paving the way for successful adaptation to change.

Key Takeaways

- The pace of change is accelerating, primarily due to technological advancements, and understanding this dynamic is vital for efficient adaptation. The concept of Moore's Law demonstrates this rapid pace in the tech industry, but the principle is applicable across multiple domains.
- Adapting to the digital age is not optional but a necessity. Technological advancements have dramatically changed our lives, offering numerous benefits but also presenting significant challenges. Embracing disruption and innovation is critical for growth and survival in the digital era.

- Understanding and managing time is crucial when managing change. As a constant resource, how we utilize time significantly impacts our capacity to adapt to change.

- Adopting mindfulness helps us recognize and understand ongoing changes, facilitating more informed decision-making and reducing stress during the adaptation process.

- A commitment to continuous learning is vital in our rapidly evolving world. However, learning should be viewed as an ongoing journey of exploration, not a race against time.

- Resilience and flexibility play pivotal roles in effective adaptation. They allow us to bounce back from setbacks and adjust our strategies, enabling us to navigate change with less friction.

- Strong support systems are significant sources of strength during times of change. These networks provide guidance, encouragement, and resources needed for effective adaptation.

- A growth mindset is critical to embracing change. Viewing challenges as opportunities for learning and growth opens our minds to new possibilities and encourages us to step out of our comfort zones.

- Time management and balance in the digital age are critical. Without losing oneself in digital tools, it's essential to establish healthy boundaries and create balance, maximizing the benefits of these tools while minimizing their potential downsides.

- Reflecting on our relationship with technology and time can provide valuable insights into our behaviors, preferences, and areas for improvement. Being intentional with our technology use and time management can facilitate more efficient adaptation to change.

CHAPTER 4

Stages and Cycles of Change

C hange is not linear but a complex web of interconnected elements, and understanding its stages and cycles allows us
to move forward with grace and adaptability. In this chapter, we'll explore the stages and cycles of change, discovering the
dynamic process that shapes our personal and professional lives.
First, a note: we're tweaking our previous format as we step into
this chapter. While the modus operandi of *The Power of Change*
has been to finish the chapters with exercises, this time, you'll find
them interspersed throughout the text. This isn't merely for vari-
ation's sake; it's deliberate and purposeful.

As we examine the multifaceted stages of change, these exercises,
positioned right where they're most potent, will act as reflective
pit stops. They ground us, allowing immediate introspection,
making our experience with change all the more tangible and impactful. The chapter takes a deeper look at the change process,
unveiling the different stages of transition that we encounter
when embracing change. Each stage offers unique challenges and
promises, and discerning our position within this transformative
journey equips us to craft more enlightened decisions. We also
tune into the emotions of change. Emotions are often underval-
ued, but we know they are central players on this stage of change,
deserving of our acknowledgment and consideration. Resistance

is also something that takes the spotlight here. It's a natural and often unsettling companion to change. Rooted in our fears, the unknown, and a fondness for the familiar, understanding resistance is our key to easing its grip. As we acquaint ourselves with its nuances, we can move through the change process with greater finesse.

When we truly embrace change, it's about capturing and using its inherent momentum, spotlighting the opportunities embedded in its cycles. These are our gateways to transformation and growth.

As we work through this chapter, imagine the exercises as the stepping stones guiding your path. Embrace the transformative power of change, and let the stages and cycles be your compass, directing you toward a more purposeful, resilient self.

Unveiling the Stages of the Change Process

Change, the ever-present force that shapes our lives, is not a singular event but a dynamic process that unfolds in distinct stages of transition. Here, we are striving to make sense of the complexities of the change process, examining each stage that marks our growth and evolution.

Acknowledging the Catalysts of Change

The change process often begins with catalysts that thrust us out of our comfort zones. Catalysts can take various forms—they might be external factors such as technological advancements, economic shifts, global events, or internal developments like personal growth and reflection. These catalysts push us to acknowledge the need for change and prompt us to begin a transformation.

Denial and Resistance: The First Hurdles

As we encounter any initial signs of change, it is common to experience denial and resistance. Denial serves as a protective mechanism, shielding us from the discomfort of facing the unfamiliar. Resistance, on the other hand, arises from fear of the unknown, concern for stability, and attachment to the status quo. In this stage, recognizing and acknowledging these emotions is essential for progress.

Exploration and Acceptance: Embracing the Possibilities

In the exploration stage, we venture into the unknown, seeking possibilities and potential opportunities. It is a time of learning, questioning, and embracing curiosity. As we gather insights and gain knowledge about the changes ahead, acceptance gradually settles in. Acceptance does not imply passive submission but an active acknowledgment of the present reality and an openness to embrace the journey of change.

Experimentation and Learning: Taking Steps Forward

Once acceptance takes root, experimentation and learning become the guiding principles. We take small steps forward, testing new approaches and gathering feedback. This stage is marked by an openness to learn from mistakes and setbacks, acknowledging that they are valuable stepping stones toward growth. Experimentation fosters creativity and encourages us to adapt and iterate in the face of change.

Integration and Transformation: Embracing the New Normal

As we move through the stages of transition, the integration of change becomes evident in our thoughts, behaviors, and actions. Transformation takes root, and what was once unfamiliar begins to feel like the new normal. This stage embodies the essence of growth and evolution as we align our identities and aspirations with the emerging landscape shaped by change.

Consolidation and Momentum: Building Resilience

Consolidation signifies the establishment of a strong foundation for continued growth. The momentum gained through maneuvering the change process moves us forward, empowering us to face future challenges with resilience. In this stage, we draw upon our learnings and experiences, building upon them to tackle new opportunities and adversities.

Reflection and Renewal: Embracing Continuous Change

The change process is a cyclical journey rather than a linear one. Reflection becomes an integral part of the cycle, allowing us to draw wisdom from our experiences and renew our commitment to embrace continuous change. Through reflection, we refine our understanding of the stages of transition, deepening our capacity to maneuver through future changes with greater insight and self-awareness.

Exercise: Your Map to Managing Change

To solidify our understanding of the change process, let us begin our first exercise—this one will help you begin to map your experiences.

- Take a moment to reflect on a significant change you have experienced.
- Identify the catalysts that triggered the change and consider the emotions that surfaced during the initial stages.
- Explore the moments of experimentation, learning, and transformation that led you to the present stage of integration and consolidation.
- Finally, reflect on the lessons learned and consider how

this experience will shape your approach to embracing future changes.

As we continue on our journey of embracing change, understanding the stages of transition helps us understand that the change process is not to be feared but embraced. It is through change that we discover the full extent of our potential and capacity for resilience. With open hearts and minds, we embark on a transformative voyage that enables us to thrive in an ever-evolving world.

Exploring the Emotional Journey Through the Ups and Downs of Change

Change is not solely a rational process; it's also an emotional journey that takes us through a range of feelings and experiences. Let's talk about the emotional landscape of change, acknowledging that there are ups and downs that accompany the transformational process. By understanding the importance of our emotions, we can become more self-aware and self-compassionate, paving the way for personal and professional growth.

Embracing Uncertainty: The Rollercoaster of Emotions

When we begin to experience change, uncertainty becomes our constant companion. We ride a rollercoaster of emotions, experiencing excitement, anticipation, fear, and anxiety all at once. It's natural to waver between moments of hope and moments of doubt, unsure of what the future holds. Embracing uncertainty is not about suppressing these emotions but acknowledging them as valid responses to change. By embracing the full spectrum of our feelings, we gain a deeper understanding of ourselves and become more resilient in the face of uncertainty.

The Tug of the Familiar: Nostalgia and Resistance

Amidst change, we may find ourselves drawn back to the familiar, even if it no longer serves us. Nostalgia for the past can be powerful, evoking a sense of comfort and safety. However, this emotional attachment to the familiar can also act as a barrier to progress, fueling resistance to the changes at hand. Acknowledging the draw of the past is essential, as it allows us to make conscious choices and cultivate openness to embrace the new.

Grief and Loss: Letting Go and Moving Forward

Change often involves letting go of what was, leading to feelings of grief and loss. Whether it's saying goodbye to familiar routines, relationships, or identities, working through these emotions is a significant part of the emotional journey. It's essential to give ourselves space to mourn the aspects of our lives that are changing, honoring the significance they held. In doing so, we create room for new possibilities and growth.

Celebrating Progress: Acknowledging Milestones

Amidst the challenges of change, it's crucial to celebrate progress and acknowledge the milestones achieved. Celebrations not only foster a positive emotional atmosphere but also reinforce the belief that change is an opportunity for growth. Recognizing our efforts and accomplishments, no matter how small, nurtures a sense of pride and fuels our motivation to keep moving forward.

Fostering Resilience: Cultivating Emotional Strength

Resilience is not about avoiding negative emotions but building the emotional strength to regulate them effectively. It involves developing healthy coping mechanisms and support systems that help us rebound from setbacks. Engaging in self-care practices, seeking support from loved ones, or seeking professional guidance can play a significant role in fostering emotional resilience.

By embracing and processing our emotions, we cultivate the emotional foundation needed to react to change with grace and adaptability.

Acceptance and Adaptation: Embracing the Present Moment

During the emotional journey of change, acceptance becomes a guiding principle. Acceptance does not imply resignation but an active embrace of the present moment. By accepting the reality of change, we can release the burden of resisting what cannot be altered and focus our energy on adapting and thriving in new circumstances.

Gratitude and Positivity: Cultivating a Positive Mindset

Practicing gratitude and adopting a positive mindset can significantly influence our experiences with change. Gratitude helps us focus on what we have, fostering a sense of abundance rather than scarcity. A positive mindset enables us to see challenges as opportunities for growth and view change as a catalyst for positive transformation.

Exercise: Embracing Your Emotional Journey

To deepen our understanding, let's engage in an exercise to embrace our emotions in times of change:

- Take a moment to reflect on a recent change you experienced.
- Explore the emotions you encountered along the way and identify the ups and downs of your emotional journey.
- Think: how did you respond to uncertainty, nostalgia, and grief?

- What strategies did you use to foster resilience and embrace the present moment?
- Finally, consider how you can cultivate gratitude and a positive mindset to support your emotional well-being during future changes.

As we embrace change, we discover the power of self-compassion and emotional awareness. The ups and downs of change become integral to our growth and personal evolution, allowing us to face future changes with greater wisdom and grace. By acknowledging and processing our emotions, we open the door to resilience and embrace change as a profound opportunity for personal and professional transformation.

Managing Resistance at Each Stage: Strategies for Progress

Resistance is an inherent aspect of the change process, presenting itself at every stage. Let's explore the various forms of resistance and uncover strategies to handle them effectively. By understanding the psychology of resistance and adopting purposeful approaches, we can transform resistance into a catalyst for progress and growth.

Recognizing the Faces of Resistance

Resistance can manifest in numerous ways, each with its unique challenges and implications. At the initial stage of denial and resistance, it may present itself as skepticism or a reluctance to accept the need for change. As we explore and experiment, resistance may take the form of doubt, fear of failure, or a desire to revert to familiar habits. In the integration and consolidation stage, resistance might surface as a reluctance to fully embrace the new normal, clinging to remnants of the past. By recognizing the various faces of resistance, we gain insight into its underlying drivers and can tailor our strategies accordingly.

Cultivating Self-Awareness: Triggers of Resistance

Self-awareness is a potent tool for managing resistance. By examining our thoughts, emotions, and behaviors, we can uncover the triggers that fuel resistance. Reflecting on our values, beliefs, and past experiences allows us to identify patterns of resistance that might be rooted in fear or past setbacks. As we gain clarity on our triggers, we can proactively address them, dismantling the barriers that inhibit progress.

Embracing Change Champions: Influencing Others Positively

Resistance is not limited to the individual; it can also permeate within organizations or social networks. As leaders or influencers, embracing change champions becomes vital in fostering a culture that welcomes change. Change champions are individuals who demonstrate openness to new ideas and actively support change initiatives. By aligning with change champions and influencing others positively, we create an environment where change is embraced rather than met with resistance.

Communicating with Empathy: Addressing Concerns and Anxieties

Effective communication is a powerful tool in overcoming resistance. When met with uncertainty or fear, individuals seek clarity and reassurance. As we communicate about change, adopting an empathetic approach is essential. Listening actively to concerns and anxieties and addressing them with transparency and compassion helps individuals feel heard and valued. Clear communication provides a roadmap for the change journey, instilling confidence and reducing resistance.

Framing Change as an Opportunity: The Power of Vision

Resistance often arises from a focus on the challenges and disruptions that accompany change. However, by reframing change as an opportunity for growth and progress, we can shift perspectives and inspire action. Articulating a compelling vision of the future and highlighting the benefits and positive outcomes of change generates enthusiasm and motivation. When individuals connect with a shared vision, they are more likely to overcome resistance and actively participate in the change process.

Empowering through Autonomy: Providing Agency in Change

Feeling a sense of autonomy and control is essential for individuals experiencing change. Empowering individuals to make choices and decisions within the change process fosters ownership and commitment. By involving individuals in decision-making, they feel valued and engaged, and resistance is replaced with a sense of agency and empowerment.

Flexibility and Adaptability: Embracing Agile Change

The pace of change in our dynamic world demands flexibility and adaptability. Embracing an agile approach to change acknowledges that plans may need adjustments and revisions. By remaining open to change within the change process, individuals can take command of unexpected developments with resilience and resourcefulness. Embracing the notion that change is not fixed but iterative helps individuals strategize for resistance and find innovative solutions.

Exercise: Creating an Action Plan to Address Personal Resistance

To reinforce our understanding of managing resistance, let's engage in an exercise to create an action plan to address personal resistance.

- Reflect on a specific area of change where you have encountered resistance.
- Identify the triggers of resistance and explore the emotions and beliefs associated with it.
- Consider the strategies discussed in this chapter and select the ones most aligned with your unique situation.
- Craft an action plan that involves leveraging your self-awareness, embracing change champions, and communicating with empathy.
- Outline the steps you will take to reframe change as an opportunity, empower yourself through autonomy, and embrace flexibility in your change journey.

By creating this action plan, you set a clear path toward recognizing resistance and progressing confidently through change. Embracing strategies to address resistance with empathy, vision, and adaptability helps us transcend barriers and seize opportunities for personal and professional progress.

By recognizing resistance as a natural part of change, we empower ourselves to thrive amidst the ever-evolving world.

Capitalizing on Momentum to Maximize Opportunities in the Change Cycle

Change is not a linear path; it resembles a dynamic cycle with distinct stages, each carrying the potential for growth and progress. To fully embrace the transformative power of change, we must learn to capture and use the momentum of cyclical change. By understanding the momentum and employing targeted strategies, we can optimize each stage to maximize opportunities and achieve sustainable growth.

Building on Success: Celebrating Milestones

The core of using momentum is the art of celebrating milestones and successes achieved at every stage of the change cycle. Often, in the hustle and bustle of constant change, we overlook the significance of progress. However, acknowledging and celebrating even the smallest successes can create a positive feedback loop that fuels our motivation and self-belief. Celebrations remind us of our capabilities and the progress we have made. When we recognize our achievements and build upon them, we create an upward spiral of momentum that thrusts us forward with renewed enthusiasm and confidence.

The Butterfly Effect: Small Actions, Big Impact

Within the change cycle, even seemingly small actions can set off a chain reaction with profound consequences. This phenomenon, known as the butterfly effect, exemplifies the interconnectedness of actions and outcomes. By recognizing the potential impact of each decision and action, we approach the change process with greater intention and mindfulness. The choices we make and the actions we take hold the power to create ripple effects in our lives and the lives of others. Embracing the butterfly effect encourages us to consider the consequences of our actions and make purposeful choices that align with our vision for positive change.

Embracing Learning Opportunities: Transformative Insights

Throughout the change cycle, we encounter numerous learning opportunities that expand our knowledge and understanding. Embracing these opportunities allows us to grow intellectually and emotionally. A growth mindset enables us to view challenges as stepping stones to new insights and personal development. By embracing learning, we extract transformative insights from our experiences, enriching our change journey, fostering resilience, and strengthening our capacity to handle future challenges with grace and adaptability.

Seizing the Flow State: Fostering Creativity

The flow state, often associated with peak performance and creativity, is a state of complete immersion and focus in an activity. Maximizing momentum involves tapping into this state, where we feel fully engaged and in sync with the task at hand. When we find activities that spark our passion and creativity, we unlock our full potential and inspire innovation throughout the change cycle. Flow experiences fuel our energy and enthusiasm, enabling us to tackle challenges with heightened focus and effectiveness. By seeking opportunities that foster flow, we create an environment that nurtures our creative abilities and maximizes our potential for growth and achievement.

Collaboration: Leveraging Support Networks

As we work through the change cycle, collaboration plays a crucial role in maximizing opportunities. Leveraging support networks and collaborative partnerships can provide fresh perspectives and insights. Engaging with diverse viewpoints fosters innovation and expands our ability to seize opportunities effectively. By actively seeking and valuing collaborative input, we create an ecosystem of shared growth and success.

The collective wisdom of a supportive network can help us overcome challenges and identify innovative solutions that may have eluded us on our own.

Integrating Feedback: Continuous Improvement

Feedback is a valuable tool for continuous improvement. Throughout the change cycle, seeking feedback from trusted sources allows us to identify blind spots and refine our approach. By embracing constructive feedback with humility and openness, we enhance our ability to adapt and maximize opportunities. Feedback serves as a compass, guiding us toward optimal growth and achievement. Integrating feedback into our journey fosters a culture of learning and empowers us to embrace change with flexibility and resilience.

Cultivating Resilience: Bouncing Back Stronger

Resilience is the flywheel that gathers momentum. When faced with setbacks or challenges, resilience empowers us to bounce back stronger and stay committed to our vision. Cultivating emotional and mental resilience transforms setbacks into stepping stones. It enables us to maintain our forward momentum, even in the face of adversity. By building resilience, we develop the inner strength needed to persevere and thrive throughout the change cycle.

Exercise: Creating a Momentum-Boosting Plan

To solidify the concept of momentum, let's engage in an exercise to create a momentum-boosting plan.

- Reflect on a recent milestone or success achieved during the change process.
- Consider the factors that contributed to this achievement, such as a growth mindset, collaborative efforts, or the flow state.
- Identify how you can replicate and expand upon these factors to harness momentum in future stages of the change cycle.
- Outline specific actions you will take to celebrate progress, seek learning opportunities, and integrate feedback for continuous improvement.

By crafting this momentum-boosting plan, you create a roadmap for maximizing opportunities and achieving sustainable growth throughout your change journey. As we embrace the art of using momentum, we tap into the inherent power of the change cycle. By celebrating successes, embracing learning, and fostering collaboration, we create a positive momentum that propels us forward with purpose and vigor. With resilience as our anchor, we manage challenges with grace and tenacity, unlocking the full potential of each stage in the change process. By making the most of momentum, we pave the way for sustained growth and success moving forward.

Exercise: Mapping Your Current Stage in a Change Process

In this comprehensive exercise, we will explore your current stage in a change process and gain valuable insights into your progress and challenges. By understanding where you stand in the change cycle, you can tailor your strategies and approach to take the next steps effectively.

Step 1: Reflect on Your Change Journey
Take a moment to reflect on the change you are currently experiencing or have recently undergone. It could be a personal or professional change, big or small. Consider the nature of the change, the goals you seek to achieve, and the emotions associated with this change.

Step 2: Identify the Stages of Change
Now, let's identify the different stages of change you have gone through or are currently going through. These stages may include:

1. **Initiation:** The initial awareness or realization that change is needed or happening.

2. Exploration and Experimentation: The stage where you actively explore options and experiment with different approaches.

3. Commitment and Action: The decision to commit to a specific path and take actionable steps toward change.

4. Integration and Consolidation: The phase where you integrate the change into your life or work and consolidate your efforts.

Step 3: Assess Your Progress
Next, assess your progress within each stage. Ask yourself:

- How far have I come in each stage of the change process?
- What milestones have I achieved so far?
- What challenges have I encountered, and how did I overcome them?
- What emotions have been predominant at each stage?

Step 4: Set Goals for the Next Stage
Based on your assessment, identify the next stage you are moving into. Define clear and realistic goals for this stage, keeping in mind the insights gained from your progress and challenges. Consider what actions you need to take to move forward effectively.

Step 5: Craft Your Action Plan
Craft an action plan that outlines the specific steps you will take to execute the next stage successfully. Include strategies for overcoming challenges, leveraging your strengths, and seeking support when needed. Be specific and detailed in your plan to create a roadmap for the future.

Step 6: Monitor and Adapt
As you progress through the change cycle, be attentive to any shifts or adjustments needed in your action plan. Monitor your progress

regularly, celebrate milestones achieved, and remain open to adapting your approach as necessary. Embrace the learning opportunities that arise and remain resilient in the face of obstacles.

Step 7: Reflect and Embrace Growth

Finally, take time to reflect on your change journey as you continue to move forward. Embrace the growth and transformation that the change process offers. Recognize the progress you have made, the lessons you have learned, and the strength you have gained. Celebrate your resilience and commitment to embracing change.

Remember, change is a dynamic journey, and mapping your current stage empowers you to move ahead with clarity and purpose. Embrace the opportunities for growth and transformation, and trust in your ability to thrive in the ever-evolving world.

Key Takeaways

- Change is not a linear process; it follows a cyclical nature with distinct stages, each carrying the potential for growth and progress.
- Celebrating milestones and successes at each stage builds positive momentum and propels us forward with confidence.
- Seemingly small actions can have a profound ripple effect, demonstrating the interconnectedness of our decisions and outcomes.
- Embracing learning opportunities throughout the change cycle enriches our journey and fosters resilience.

- Tapping into the flow state enhances creativity and allows us to tackle challenges with heightened focus and effectiveness.
- Collaboration leverages support networks, leading to innovative solutions and shared growth.
- Integrating feedback drives continuous improvement and guides us toward optimal growth and achievement.
- Cultivating resilience empowers us to bounce back stronger from setbacks, maintaining forward momentum.
- Through purposeful strategies, we can harness momentum and unlock the full potential of each stage in the change process.

CHAPTER 5

Overcoming Resistance to Change

I n Chapter 5, we examine one of the most complex parts of our experience with change: resistance. Resistance is the pushback from within that challenges our most fervent desires to evolve and thrive. Resistance often feels like an immovable barrier, but by understanding its origins and nuances, we can overcome its power, take charge of its momentum, and use it to move forward rather than have it hold us back.

Resistance isn't merely an obstacle; it's a mirror that reflects our deepest apprehensions, our moments of uncertainty, and our fondness for the comfort of what we know. Let's dive deep into those undercurrents to make sense of the psychology of resistance, understand our fears, and break free of the comforting embrace of our well-worn comfort zones. As with every challenge, resistance offers us invaluable lessons and opportunities.

By understanding it, we're not only preparing to face it but to use it as a launchpad. Strategies to overcome resistance are not about avoidance but engagement. It's about dialogue, not dismissal. Throughout this chapter, we'll explore these strategies, drawing up a plan to guide us past our own hesitations. But the journey doesn't end with personal understanding; it extends to influencing the world around us. As we go through these pages, we also

touch upon the art of cultivating change champions—those beacon lights who inspire, guide, and influence others to embrace the
winds of change. Their importance in our personal and professional spheres cannot be emphasized enough. We'll also build a
bridge between theory and practice with a robust exercise in reflecting and acting upon resistance. This exercise will also help
you draft your personal plan to work through resistance and capture the momentum of change to your advantage. As we take this
journey through Chapter 5, remember that resistance is not about
stagnation but movement. It indicates that we're on the brink of
something new, something transformative. Let's embrace it, understand it, and chart a path through it, emerging on the other side
with renewed purpose and energy.

Identifying and Understanding Resistance to Change

We recognize that change, though essential for growth and progress, often encounters resistance, both from within ourselves
and from those around us. By understanding the roots and complexities of this resistance, we can gain invaluable insights into the
psychological and emotional barriers that hinder our progress.
Armed with this understanding, we are better equipped to address resistance effectively and work through the change process
with confidence, purpose, and compassion.

Resistance to change is a natural human response deeply ingrained in our psychology. As creatures of habit and routine, we
seek stability and certainty to create a sense of security. When
faced with the uncertainty and ambiguity that change brings, we
instinctively react by seeking to preserve the familiar and secure
aspects of our lives.

Recognizing the universality of resistance allows us to approach it with empathy and compassion, both in ourselves and others. One of the primary drivers of resistance is the fear of the unknown. Stepping into uncharted territory can evoke anxiety and apprehension about potential risks and outcomes. This fear often manifests as a reluctance to embrace change, even when it may lead to personal and professional growth. Understanding and acknowledging this fear allows us to address it directly, reframing change as an opportunity for exploration and discovery. By embracing change with a sense of adventure, we open ourselves up to new possibilities and untapped potential. Resistance to change can also stem from a desire to avoid potential losses. Our natural inclination to preserve what we have cultivated over time can create a significant barrier to embracing new possibilities. The comfort zones we build around ourselves serve as protective shells, shielding us from uncertainty and discomfort. However, understanding that stepping outside these zones is essential for growth and expansion empowers us to challenge our own resistance and step into transformative change. Change often demands that we alter our well-established routines and habits. The disruption this entails can be unsettling, as it requires us to relearn and recalibrate our daily lives. Identifying the resistance stemming from these disruptions enables us to create supportive structures and habits that align with our change goals. By proactively integrating new habits and routines that support the change process, we pave the way for smoother transitions and increased adaptability.

Resistance can also emerge from a perceived lack of control over the change process. When we feel that change is imposed upon us without our consent or involvement, we may resist it even more vehemently. Empowering individuals to actively participate in shaping the change process cultivates a sense of ownership and agency. By involving stakeholders and soliciting their input, we foster a collaborative environment that nurtures a sense of shared responsibility for the change journey. The past holds a powerful emotional grip on our lives. Nostalgia and sentimental attachments to how things used to be can lead us to resist change as we yearn for what once was.

Embracing change involves reconciling with the past and cherishing memories but understanding that growth necessitates letting go and embracing new possibilities. By honoring the past while remaining open to the future, we strike a delicate balance that allows us to move forward with purpose and authenticity.

The Psychology of Resistance: Fear, Uncertainty, and Comfort Zones

Let's take a closer look at the psychology that underpins resistance to change. As we move forward in an ever-evolving world, we must grasp the emotional and cognitive dimensions that influence our response to change; this helps us transform resistance into an opportunity for growth and self-discovery. Let's examine these dimensions individually and then explore how we can fight back against their power and the psychology of resistance.

Fear, aka, the Elusive Foe: Fear is an innate human emotion, deeply engrained in our primal psyche. When faced with change, the fear of the unknown often emerges, preventing us from embracing new possibilities. However, understanding fear as a natural part of the change process allows us to approach it with compassion and curiosity. By acknowledging our fears and those of others, we create a safe space for vulnerability, fostering authentic connections and openness to change.

Uncertainty When Exploring New Terrain: Uncertainty accompanies change like a faithful companion, magnifying our fears and insecurities. The lack of a clear roadmap and predictable outcomes can trigger anxiety and doubt. Embracing uncertainty as an integral part of the change journey reframes it as an opportunity for exploration and self-discovery. Embracing uncertainty as an invitation to learn and grow empowers us to forge ahead with confidence, regardless of the challenges that lie ahead.

The Comfort Zone is a Tempting Refuge: Our comfort zones represent the familiar and secure aspects of our lives, shielded from the uncertainties of change. While these zones offer safety and stability, they can also hinder personal and professional growth. Stepping beyond our comfort zones may be daunting, but it is an essential step towards unlocking our true capabilities and embracing transformative change.

Strategies for Overcoming Resistance

This expansive section may be the most crucial part of the entire book. Here, we'll put resistance under the microscope to discover strategies for dismantling it and moving forward on the path to change.

These well-thought-out strategies emerge not merely as suggestions but as invaluable tools. They are designed for both individuals and larger organizational entities that are looking to get a handle on the immense potential of transformation, aiming to foster beneficial results and a forward momentum. Let's get started.

Personal Strategies for Embracing Change:

Start with Self-Reflection and Awareness: The journey of overcoming resistance to change begins with self-reflection and awareness. Take time to introspect and identify the underlying reasons for your resistance. Are you holding onto comfort and familiarity? Are you anxious about the uncertainties that change brings? By gaining clarity on your emotions and thought patterns, you can better understand the root causes of your resistance and develop targeted strategies to address them.

Cultivate a Growth Mindset: Embrace a growth mindset that views change as an opportunity for learning and improvement. Shift your perspective from seeing change as a threat to perceiving it as a chance to grow and evolve. Embrace the idea that challenges are stepping stones towards personal development. By fostering a growth mindset, you cultivate resilience and adaptability, enabling you to handle change with confidence and enthusiasm.

Set Realistic Goals: Set realistic and achievable goals to guide you through the change process. Break down the change into smaller, manageable steps, and celebrate each milestone you reach. This approach not only keeps you motivated but also helps you track your progress. Setting and achieving goals during times of change instills a sense of accomplishment, reinforcing your belief in your ability to overcome obstacles and adapt to new circumstances.

Embrace a Learning Mindset: View change as an opportunity to learn and acquire new skills. Seek out resources, workshops, and training programs that align with the changes you are facing.

Embracing a learning mindset empowers you to proactively acquire the knowledge and competencies needed to thrive in the new environment. By continuously seeking knowledge and growth, you equip yourself with the tools to overcome resistance and seize new opportunities.

Seek Support and Guidance: Reach out for support and guidance from trusted friends, mentors, or coaches. Sharing your concerns and uncertainties with others can offer valuable insights and fresh perspectives. Seek advice from individuals who have managed similar changes successfully, and learn from their experiences. A support network can provide the encouragement and motivation needed to persist through moments of resistance.

Practice Mindfulness and Self-Care: Amidst change, it is crucial to practice mindfulness and self-care. Take time for self-reflection, meditation, or relaxation exercises to stay centered and focused. Nourish your physical, emotional, and mental well-being through activities that bring you joy and tranquility. Practicing self-care not only reduces stress but also enhances your ability to adapt to change with clarity and composure.

Embrace Flexibility and Adaptability: Embrace the idea that change is constant and requires flexibility and adaptability. Embracing a flexible mindset allows you to adjust your approach to fit new circumstances and challenges. Be open to alternative solutions and be willing to pivot when necessary. By embracing flexibility, you transform resistance into an opportunity for innovation and creative problem-solving.

Visualize Success and Positive Outcomes: Visualize success and positive outcomes that can result from embracing change. Create a mental picture of yourself thriving in the new environment.

Visualization helps rewire your brain to focus on possibilities rather than fears. By envisioning success, you reinforce your belief in your ability to overcome resistance and achieve personal growth through change.

Celebrate Progress and Resilience: Acknowledge and celebrate your progress and resilience throughout the change process. Celebrating small victories and milestones boosts your confidence and motivation. Recognize the moments when you embrace change with courage and determination, and appreciate your capacity to navigate challenges with grace and resilience.

Practice Gratitude: Cultivate gratitude, even in the face of change and resistance. Take time each day to reflect on the positive aspects of the changes you are experiencing. Express gratitude for the opportunities and growth that change brings into your life. Practicing gratitude nurtures a sense of positivity and optimism, fostering a mindset that welcomes change as a gift rather than a burden.

Organizational Strategies for Driving Positive Transformation:

Engage in Open Dialogue: Open and transparent communication is the cornerstone of overcoming resistance to change. Leaders and change agents must foster an environment where employees feel encouraged to voice their concerns, questions, and uncertainties. Holding regular town hall meetings, focus groups, or one-on-one conversations allows individuals to share their perspectives and contribute to the change process. By actively listening and addressing concerns, leaders build trust and create a shared understanding of the reasons behind the change.

Communicate the Vision and Benefits: Clearly articulating the vision and benefits of the change is essential for inspiring buy-in and support. Employees need to understand the purpose behind the change and how it aligns with the organization's values and goals. Providing a compelling vision empowers individuals to see the change as an opportunity for growth and personal development. Additionally, communicating the potential benefits and positive outcomes of the change creates a sense of excitement and optimism, motivating individuals to actively embrace the transformation.

Involve Employees in the Change Process: Involving employees in the change process fosters a sense of ownership and commitment. Encourage individuals to participate in brainstorming sessions, problem-solving workshops, or pilot projects related to the change. By empowering employees to be part of the decision-making process, they become invested in the success of the change initiative. This sense of ownership leads to greater accountability and a shared responsibility for driving the desired outcomes.

Provide Adequate Training and Support: Change can bring about new roles, responsibilities, and skill requirements. Providing comprehensive training and support equips employees with the necessary knowledge and skills to thrive in the changed environment. Offering coaching, workshops, and access to resources ensures that individuals feel confident and capable during the transition. By investing in the development of employees, organizations pave the way for a smoother and more successful change journey.

Celebrate Small Wins: Recognizing and celebrating small wins along the change journey is essential for maintaining momentum and morale. Acknowledging and rewarding progress, even in the early stages of the change process, reinforces the positive impact of the transformation. Celebrations can take various forms, such as team gatherings, commendations, or acknowledgment in company-wide communications. By celebrating each milestone, individuals are motivated to continue embracing the change and working towards larger goals.

Address Resistance with Empathy: Resistance to change often stems from fear, uncertainty, or a sense of loss. Leaders and change agents should approach resistance with empathy and understanding. Taking the time to listen to individual concerns and empathize with their emotions creates a supportive environment.

Acknowledging the challenges associated with change validates personal experiences and fosters a sense of belonging within the organization. Empathy builds trust and lays the foundation for a collaborative and united approach to change.

Provide a Supportive Network: Creating a supportive network within the organization helps individuals work through the change journey with confidence. Establishing mentorship programs, peer support groups, or buddy systems allows employees to seek guidance and encouragement from their colleagues. A strong support network provides a safe space for sharing experiences, exchanging ideas, and learning from one another. By building a culture of support, organizations empower individuals to embrace change as a collective effort.

Lead by Example: Leaders play a crucial role in overcoming resistance to change. Leading by example and demonstrating a positive attitude toward change set the tone for the entire organization. Leaders should openly embrace the change, communicate their enthusiasm, and demonstrate resilience in the face of challenges. By embodying the values and behaviors they seek to cultivate, leaders inspire others to follow suit and adopt a more receptive attitude.

Monitor Progress and Adjust Accordingly: Change is a dynamic process, and adjustments may be necessary. Monitoring progress and actively seeking feedback allows organizations to identify potential roadblocks and areas for improvement.

Regularly reviewing the change strategy and making necessary adaptations ensures that the change initiative stays on track and remains relevant to the evolving needs of the organization and its employees.

Celebrate the Transformation Journey: At the culmination of the change process, celebrating the transformation journey becomes a powerful motivator for sustained growth. Recognizing and honoring the efforts of individuals and teams who embraced the change and contributed to its success reinforces the value of change as a driver of progress. By commemorating the transformation journey, organizations instill a culture of continuous improvement and a commitment to embracing change as an integral part of their path to success.

As we wrap up our deep dive into strategies for overcoming resistance, it becomes clear that managing and succeeding through change is both a personal and collective endeavor. The narrative underscores the imperative of self-awareness, emphasizing the power of introspection, goal-setting, and the pursuit of continuous learning. This holds true for all individuals and organizations working toward a transformative change. Empathy, communication, support, and resilience are the keys to embracing change and moving confidently forward. We must all use our emotional intelligence and willingness to stay open-minded to help ourselves and each other through the oft-worrying stages of change.

Within organizations, it is essential to establish change management strategies that account for the psychological aspects of change resistance. These strategies should be tailored to address the specific challenges faced by employees and teams at different stages of the change process. By proactively identifying and managing resistance, leaders can prevent potential roadblocks and ensure a smoother transition.

Cultivating Change Champions: Influencing Others to Embrace Change

Next, we'll look into the strategies and qualities that make change champions influential in guiding others through the process of embracing change.

Change champions play a vital role in creating a positive and adaptive culture that welcomes transformation as an opportunity for growth and innovation. By cultivating change champions within organizations, we foster an environment where individuals are empowered to manage change with confidence, enthusiasm, and resilience.

What are the defining characteristics of a champion for change?

1. They Lead with Authenticity
Change champions understand the significance of leading by example and embodying the change they advocate for. They are authentic in their approach, demonstrating genuine enthusiasm for

the transformation. Authenticity inspires trust and credibility, as individuals can relate to someone who is genuine and transparent. Change champions openly share their own experiences with change, including the challenges and growth they encountered. By authentically embracing the change themselves, change champions inspire others to follow suit and adopt a positive attitude toward the upcoming challenges and opportunities.

2. They Communicate with Clarity and Purpose

Effective communication is vital in influencing others to embrace change. Change champions articulate the vision and goals of the transformation with clarity and purpose. They craft compelling narratives that illustrate the potential benefits of the change and its alignment with the organization's mission and values.

Communicating with clarity and purpose enables individuals to understand the reasons behind the change and its significance in the organization's larger purpose. Through clear and consistent communication, change champions instill a sense of purpose and direction, inspiring individuals to embrace the change journey wholeheartedly.

3. They Listen and Empathize

Change champions recognize that change can evoke a range of emotions in individuals. They are empathetic listeners who create a safe space for open dialogue. When individuals express their concerns, fears, and uncertainties about the change, change champions listen attentively and validate their emotions.

By genuinely understanding and addressing these concerns, change champions build trust and cultivate a supportive environment. Empathetic listening fosters a sense of belonging and psychological safety, allowing individuals to express their thoughts and feelings without judgment. It also provides valuable insights into the sources of resistance, enabling change champions to develop targeted strategies for addressing them.

4. They Collaborate and Encourage Participation

Change champions foster a collaborative culture where individuals are encouraged to actively participate in the change process. They recognize that involving employees in decision-making empowers them and creates a sense of ownership and commitment. Change champions create opportunities for brainstorming, idea-sharing, and problem-solving sessions, where employees can contribute their insights and perspectives.

By involving others in the change process, change champions create a sense of ownership and commitment to the transformation. This collaborative approach fosters a feeling of empowerment and encourages individuals to take an active role in shaping the organization's future.

5. They Recognize and Celebrate Progress

Acknowledging and celebrating progress, no matter how small is a vital aspect of being a change champion. Change journeys can be challenging, and recognizing individual and team achievements during the change process reinforces positive behavior and motivates others to continue embracing the transformation. Celebrations can take various forms, such as public recognition, team gatherings, or acknowledgment in company-wide communications. By celebrating each milestone, change champions instill a sense of accomplishment and encourage a collective effort toward achieving larger goals. Celebrations also serve as an opportunity to reflect on the positive impact of the change and reinforce the organization's commitment to embracing change as a catalyst for growth.

6. They Provide Support and Guidance

Change champions extend unwavering support and guidance to colleagues facing challenges during the change process. They act as mentors or coaches, offering encouragement, insights, and practical assistance. Providing a solid support system helps individuals handle the change with confidence and resilience. By being accessible and approachable, change champions create an atmosphere of trust where individuals feel comfortable seeking help and guidance when needed. They are committed to helping others overcome obstacles and develop the skills and mindset necessary to navigate change successfully.

7. They Embrace Continuous Learning

Change champions emphasize the value of continuous learning and personal growth. They inspire others to view change as an opportunity for acquiring new skills and knowledge. By fostering a learning mindset, individuals become better equipped to adapt to the evolving landscape and take on new responsibilities with confidence. Change champions actively seek opportunities for their own growth and share their learning experiences with others, inspiring a culture of curiosity and development within the organization. They encourage individuals to invest in their own development, whether through workshops, courses, or self-directed learning.

8. They Address Resistance with Patience

Resistance to change is natural and expected. Change champions address resistance with patience and understanding. They acknowledge and validate individual concerns and provide reassurance, helping individuals manage their apprehensions and embrace the transformation positively. By demonstrating patience and empathy, change champions create an environment where individuals feel supported and encouraged to move past their resistance towards a more receptive attitude to change. They take the time to listen to individual concerns and offer thoughtful responses that acknowledge the challenges associated with change.

9. Share Success Stories

Change champions share success stories of individuals or teams who have successfully embraced the change and achieved positive outcomes. These stories are powerful examples that inspire and motivate others to follow suit. Success stories highlight the benefits of the change and the transformative effects it can have on individuals and teams.

By showcasing real-life examples, change champions foster optimism and confidence in others, helping them envision their own successful transformation journey. Sharing success stories reinforces the belief that change is attainable, inspiring individuals to persevere through challenges and stay committed to the change journey.

10. Foster a Positive Change Culture

Above all, change champions play a vital role in fostering a positive change culture within organizations. They actively promote an environment where change is viewed as an opportunity for growth and innovation rather than a disruption or threat.

By embracing change as an integral part of the organization's evolution, change champions inspire others to develop a flexible and adaptive mindset, encouraging everyone to proactively embrace new possibilities and seize opportunities for personal and professional growth. They create a culture that values learning, collaboration, and continuous improvement, laying the foundation for an organization that thrives in the ever-evolving world.

Here are some ways you can be a change champion:

- **Share Personal Experiences:** Change champions openly share their own experiences with change, including both successes and challenges. By sharing personal stories, they demonstrate vulnerability and create a relatable connection with others.

- **Admit Mistakes and Learn from Them:** Authentic leaders acknowledge their mistakes and take responsibility for them. They use these moments as opportunities for growth and learning, showing others that it's okay to make mistakes and that growth comes from embracing them.

- **Be Transparent:** Transparency is essential in building trust. Change champions are open and honest about the reasons behind the change, the challenges that may arise, and the expected outcomes. Transparent communication fosters a culture of openness and builds confidence in the change process.

- **Craft a Compelling Vision:** Change champions articulate a clear and compelling vision of the desired future state. They communicate the benefits and opportunities that the change will bring, inspiring others to see the positive impact of the transformation.

- **Use Simple and Understandable Language:** Avoid jargon or complex language that might confuse or alienate others. Change champions communicate in simple and understandable terms, making it easy for everyone to grasp the key messages.

- ***Provide Context and Relevance:*** Help individuals see how the change aligns with the organization's mission and values. Explain how the transformation relates to the broader goals and how it contributes to the overall success of the organization.

- ***Active Listening:*** Change champions practice active listening by giving their full attention to others when they speak. They avoid interrupting and show genuine interest in understanding the perspectives of those experiencing the change.

- ***Validate Emotions:*** When individuals express their concerns or fears, change champions validate their emotions. They acknowledge that change can be challenging and that it's normal to feel uncertain or anxious. By validating emotions, change champions create a safe space for open communication.

- ***Put Yourself in Their Shoes:*** Empathetic leaders try to understand the emotions and thoughts of others by putting themselves in their shoes. They consider the impact of the change on individuals' lives and empathize with their unique situations.

- ***Seek Input and Feedback:*** Change champions actively seek input and feedback from employees and stakeholders. They encourage individuals to share their ideas, suggestions, and concerns, making them feel valued and heard.

- ***Involve Employees in Decision-Making:*** Change champions involve employees in decision-making processes related to the change. This participative approach empowers individuals to contribute insights and shape the organization's future.

- *Recognize and Appreciate Contributions:* When individuals participate in the change process, change champions acknowledge and appreciate their contributions. Recognizing efforts reinforces positive behavior and encourages others to actively engage in the change journey.

- *Create Collaborative Spaces:* Change champions create collaborative spaces for brainstorming, problem-solving, and idea-sharing. These spaces foster a culture of collaboration and teamwork, where individuals feel encouraged to participate and contribute to the change initiative.

Cultivating change champions is a transformative endeavor that shapes the culture of an organization. By cultivating change champions, either yourself or others, we pave the way for an organization that thrives in a fast-paced world, seizing opportunities for growth and driving sustainable success.

Now, let's turn our focus from the abstract to the tangible. As we've done in other chapters, we can examine case studies to see the power of change in action. What better way to illuminate the complexities of resistance than to explore a titan of the tech world, a company that once faced significant hurdles and had to reinvent itself in the face of change? Let's examine the incredible evolution of Microsoft, a company that, staring down monumental resistance, managed to redefine itself in an era of digital transformation.

Case Study: Microsoft's Shift to Cloud Computing

Introduction: By the mid-2010s, technology giant Microsoft stood at a crucial juncture. The traditional software sales model, involving one-time license purchases, was becoming outdated. The future was in cloud computing and subscription services. To stay relevant, Microsoft needed to undergo a massive transformation. But shifting from their conventional model to the cloud was not just about technology; it was about managing human resistance to this change.

Background: Satya Nadella took over as CEO of Microsoft in 2014, inheriting a company steeped in its past successes but facing an uncertain future. Cloud computing, led by companies like Amazon, was changing the software landscape. Microsoft, with its significant employee base, had to realign its business model, culture, and product offerings.

Identifying and Understanding Resistance: Not all employees were on board with this seismic shift. Many questioned the profitability of the cloud model. Others, especially those involved in traditional software development and sales, feared job redundancies.

The Psychology of Resistance: At Microsoft, the resistance was rooted in:

- **Fear** of the unknown – "What does a cloud-first Microsoft look like?"
- **Uncertainty** about job security and roles.
- **Comfort Zones** - Employees had enjoyed years, if not decades, of success with the previous model.

Nadella and his leadership team implemented several strategies:

- **Open Communication**: Nadella frequently communicated the vision of a cloud-first company and the reasons behind it.
- **Training and Skill Development**: To ease uncertainties, Microsoft invested heavily in training its workforce in cloud technologies.
- **Inclusive Decision-making**: Departments were involved in the transformation process, ensuring they had a stake in the new direction.

Cultivating Change Champions: Nadella identified and promoted individuals who were enthusiastic about the cloud model. These 'Change Champions' played pivotal roles in their respective departments, influencing their colleagues to understand and embrace the cloud vision.

Exercise in Practice: A group of employees from the traditional software sales team took the initiative to understand their personal resistance. Using the action plan, they recognized their fears and hesitations. By engaging in discussions with the change champions and undergoing cloud-based training sessions, they pivoted their roles to align with Microsoft's new direction.

Outcome: Microsoft's successful transition to a cloud-first company is evident today, with Azure, its cloud platform, becoming one of the leading players in the market. Their subscription model, Office 365, boasts millions of users. The company not only maintained its relevance but also expanded its market presence, all while managing and mitigating internal resistance.

Addendum: Beyond the Cloud - AI and Leadership at Microsoft

The journey of Microsoft under Nadella's leadership is not just confined to cloud computing. It also extends into the field of AI and reflects a unique leadership style shaped by personal experiences. Nadella's approach, influenced by his son Zain's life and challenges, emphasizes a growth mindset. This philosophy, encouraging continuous self-questioning and adaptability, has been pivotal in steering Microsoft's strategies. Under Nadella, Microsoft has advanced significantly in the AI revolution, surpassing giants like Google and Amazon. This success is not only a testament to technological innovation but also to a leadership style that values resilience, constant learning, and the ability to embrace change. Nadella's personal and professional experiences have intertwined to shape a future-focused Microsoft, adept in navigating the complexities of both cloud computing and artificial intelligence.

Conclusion: Microsoft's story underlines that technological evolution is deeply intertwined with the human aspects of change. From cloud computing to AI, the company's journey offers valuable insights into overcoming resistance and fostering a culture of innovation and adaptability. Nadella's leadership exemplifies how personal experiences can inform and enhance professional success, guiding an organization through significant transformations.

From the technology hubs of the American West to the bustling corridors of European corporations and the dynamic business landscape of Southeast Asia, overcoming resistance to change is not constrained by geography or industry. Just as Microsoft grappled with internal and external shifts, other global leaders have faced their unique challenges head-on. Let's briefly examine the stories of Paul Polman of Unilever and Tony Fernandes of AirAsia. These two visionaries did not take the same path to change, yet both men's journeys resonate with the universal themes of persistence, vision, and transformation.

Paul Polman's Sustainable Revolution at Unilever

In the world of fast-moving consumer goods (FMCG), where the primary focus has traditionally been quarterly results and short-term profitability, Paul Polman stood out as a visionary leader determined to reshape the landscape. When he took the helm of Unilever in 2009, he began steering this colossal ship in a direction that many in the industry found both ambitious and, to some degree, risky. Polman's vision was centered on sustainability. He believed in a business model where companies didn't just make profits but also had a positive impact on the world. He introduced the Unilever Sustainable Living Plan, aiming to decouple the company's growth from its environmental footprint while increasing its positive social impact.

This was a grand vision: halve the environmental impact of products, enhance the health and well-being of over a billion people, and improve the livelihoods of millions by 2020. The initial reaction to Polman's plans was mixed. Investors, accustomed to the traditional profit-first mantra, were skeptical. Focusing on long-term sustainability in a market driven by short-term goals and quarterly performance reviews was counterintuitive to many. But Polman was undeterred. In a move that shocked many, he abolished quarterly reporting, signaling a clear shift from short-termism. He declared, "Put your money elsewhere if you don't "buy into this long-term value-creation model, which is equitable, which is shared, which is sustainable." His time at Unilever demonstrated the practicality of his vision. Under Polman's leadership, the company's sustainable brands grew 50% faster than the rest of the business and delivered more than 60% of the company's growth by his last year. Moreover, Polman's insistence on sustainability didn't merely translate into an environmental stance. He aimed to make Unilever a beacon of purposeful business, emphasizing employee welfare, diversity, and inclusion.

When Polman stepped down in 2018, he left a legacy of transformation. Unilever had been steered towards becoming a company that was not only profitable but also responsible, sustainable, and forward-thinking. Paul Polman's journey at Unilever exemplifies the blend of vision and resilience. It demonstrates that even in traditional corporate structures, with the right leadership, it's possible to overcome resistance and institute transformative change.

Tony Fernandes and the AirAsia Turnaround

When one thinks of game-changing entrepreneurs from Southeast Asia, Tony Fernandes is a name that invariably tops the list. This charismatic leader's story with AirAsia is a testament to the power of vision, tenacity, and the ability to effect real change. In 2001, Fernandes, along with a few partners, took over AirAsia, an ailing airline with just two planes, twenty staff, and a whopping debt of $11 million. The aviation industry was in turmoil, further compounded by the aftermath of the 9/11 attacks. Many would deem this acquisition a folly, but Fernandes saw an opportunity. He envisioned making air travel accessible to everyone, transforming the very essence of what it means to fly in Southeast Asia. From the outset, resistance to his ideas was palpable. Critics doubted the feasibility of a low-cost airline model in a region dominated by state-owned carriers. Employees, accustomed to a traditional airline model, were skeptical of Fernandes's drastic changes, which included ticketless travel and no-frills service. Fernandes, however, remained resolute. He believed in the principle: "If you make the pie bigger, everyone can have a slice."

His philosophy was straightforward—by keeping operational costs at a minimum and passing those savings to the consumers, air travel could be democratized. He introduced radical shifts in the airline's operations. Traditional practices were overhauled, processes were streamlined, and a culture of innovation was fostered. He also took the unconventional approach of directly engaging with customers and staff. This feedback-driven model ensured that the airline continuously evolved to meet its customers' needs. His leadership style was infectious. Leading from the front, he was open to rolling up his sleeves and working alongside his team, whether serving at check-in counters or handling baggage.

This hands-on approach, combined with his genuine commitment to both staff welfare and customer satisfaction, slowly won over internal skeptics. Under Fernandes's leadership, AirAsia underwent a remarkable transformation. From its modest beginnings, the airline grew exponentially. By 2019, AirAsia had flown over 600 million passengers, boasting a fleet of more than 250 aircraft and operating more than 1,400 flights daily to over 150 destinations. Tony Fernandes's AirAsia story underscores the value of a clear vision, relentless determination, and the ability to challenge the status quo. In overcoming the inherent resistance to change, Fernandes not only transformed an airline but redefined air travel for an entire region.

Exercise: Creating an Action Plan to Address Personal Resistance

It's time to begin taking action. In this transformative exercise, we will focus on creating a personalized action plan to address and overcome personal resistance to change. Recognizing that resistance is a natural part of the change process, this exercise empowers you to proactively manage your emotions and thoughts and develop strategies to embrace change as a catalyst for growth and fulfillment.

Step 1: Reflect on Your Resistance

Take a moment for self-reflection and introspection. Identify specific areas or aspects of the change that trigger resistance within you. Ask yourself questions such as:

- What emotions do I experience when faced with this change?
- What beliefs or assumptions are driving my resistance?
- Are there any past experiences influencing my current response to change?

Understanding the root causes of your resistance is a crucial step in developing targeted strategies to address them.

Step 2: Identify Personal Growth Goals

Consider the potential opportunities for personal growth and development that this change presents. What skills or competencies could you acquire or enhance through embracing this transformation? Write down specific goals related to personal growth that you want to achieve during this change process.

Step 3: Cultivate a Growth Mindset

Embrace a growth mindset that views change as an opportunity for learning and improvement. Challenge any fixed beliefs or limiting thoughts that may be holding you back. Replace them with empowering affirmations that encourage adaptability and resilience.

Step 4: Create a Support System
Build a support network of individuals who can offer encouragement, guidance, and understanding throughout the change process. Reach out to friends, mentors, or colleagues who have successfully undergone similar changes. Their insights and experiences can provide valuable perspectives to help you overcome resistance.

Step 5: Set Actionable Steps
Break down the change into actionable steps that align with your personal growth goals. Consider the following:

- What specific actions can you take to embrace this change?
- How can you build new skills or competencies related to the change?
- What resources or support do you need to overcome resistance effectively?

Write down these actionable steps in a clear and organized manner.

Step 6: Visualize Success
Create a mental picture of yourself thriving in the changed environment. Visualize how you confidently handle the challenges and opportunities that arise. Embrace the positive outcomes that can result from embracing the change. Visualization helps rewire your brain to focus on possibilities and instills a sense of belief in your ability to overcome resistance.

Step 7: Monitor Progress and Adjust
Regularly review your action plan and monitor your progress. Celebrate the milestones and progress you make along the way. Be open to adjusting your plan if needed, as change is a dynamic

process. Stay flexible and adaptable, and continue to take steps towards embracing the change.

Step 8: Celebrate Your Growth

As you work through the change process and overcome resistance, celebrate your personal growth and achievements. Recognize the moments when you embrace change with courage and determination. Acknowledge the positive changes in your mindset and behavior. By creating this action plan and committing to addressing personal resistance, you empower yourself to embrace change as a journey of personal growth and self-discovery. Embracing the opportunities within change allows you to thrive in an ever-evolving world and unlock your full potential. Remember, you have the strength and capacity to navigate change with resilience and confidence.

Key Takeaways

- Overcoming resistance to change requires self-reflection and awareness of the emotions and beliefs driving resistance.
- Cultivating a growth mindset empowers us to view change as an opportunity for learning and personal development.
- Setting clear and realistic goals for personal growth helps guide us through the change process.
- Building a support network of trusted individuals offers valuable guidance and encouragement.
- Developing actionable steps aligned with our growth goals allows us to proactively embrace the change.
- Visualization helps us rewire our brains to focus on positive outcomes and reinforce our belief in overcoming resistance.

- Regularly monitoring progress and adjusting the action plan ensures adaptability throughout the change journey.
- Celebrating our personal growth and achievements encourages a positive attitude towards embracing change.

CHAPTER 6

Change and AI

I n an era where change is the only constant, Artificial Intelligence (AI) has emerged as a groundbreaking force. As AI becomes entwined in all aspects of business and society, it brings opportunities, challenges, and ethical considerations—all of which must be grappled with as we learn to live in an AI-driven world. In this chapter, we'll explore insights into using AI responsibly, ensuring both individual and organizational readiness for a world where machines and minds collaborate more closely than ever.

The Rise of Artificial Intelligence: Understanding the Impact on Society and Workplaces

In the course of human development, we've encountered many changes, from the rise of fire to the birth of the Internet. Each transformation has asked us to adapt, to innovate, and, above all, to change. Now, as we stand on the brink of a new era, we are again asked to make space for something new—the rise of Artificial Intelligence (AI). Let's explore the phenomenon of AI, its widespread implications on our society and workplaces, and how we, as resilient human beings, can accept and embrace this new reality.

The Advent of AI: Tracing its Origins and Progress

The inception of AI can be traced back to the mid-20th century when scientists began to envision machines that could mimic human intelligence. It was a dream that seemed far-fetched, but relentless research, unprecedented technological advancements, and a never-ending human drive to innovate have turned this dream into a reality.

Today, we are surrounded by AI; it assists us in our homes, powers our online experiences, and even drives our cars. Over the decades, AI has progressed from basic rule-based systems to advanced machine learning and deep learning models capable of adapting based on experience, recognizing patterns, and making predictions.

From defeating world champions in chess to diagnosing diseases with impressive accuracy, AI has demonstrated capabilities once thought to be exclusively human.

The Societal Impacts of AI: A New Social Order

AI's impact on society is multifaceted and profound. It's paving the way for smart cities where AI manages traffic flow, predicts infrastructure needs, and improves emergency responses. In healthcare, AI algorithms are assisting doctors in diagnosing diseases and personalizing treatment plans. In education, AI-powered adaptive learning platforms are providing personalized learning experiences, revolutionizing the way we teach and learn.

Amidst these transformative changes, we must also acknowledge the challenges. Issues of privacy and security, biases in AI systems, and the digital divide are all significant societal concerns that need to be addressed. We need to ensure that AI is used responsibly, ethically, and for the benefit of all.

The Workplace Revolution: AI and the Future of Work

AI is also transforming our workplaces, automating routine tasks and freeing up human workers to focus on more complex and creative tasks. From autonomous vehicles to AI chatbots, technology is reshaping job roles and industries.

This transformative power of AI brings with it a twofold challenge. Firstly, we must deal with the fear of job displacement due to automation. While AI will undoubtedly replace some jobs, it's essential to remember that it will also create new ones. Secondly, there's a shift in skill requirements. As AI takes over routine tasks, there's a growing need for advanced cognitive skills and emotional intelligence in the workforce.

Embracing the Change: Leveraging AI for Societal and Organizational Growth

Change is often accompanied by uncertainty and resistance. However, the key to thriving in this AI era is embracing the change. By understanding AI's capabilities, potential, and limitations, we can leverage it for societal and organizational growth. We need to foster a learning culture where curiosity is rewarded, and continuous learning is a norm. Only then can we prepare ourselves and our workforce for this AI-driven world. It's not just about learning to code or understanding AI algorithms. It's also about developing the skills AI can't replicate – critical thinking, creativity, empathy, and leadership. Furthermore, organizations must proactively adapt to this change. This involves integrating AI into their operations, investing in the right talent and technology, and aligning their strategies with an AI-powered future.

Living and Thriving in an AI World

The rise of AI represents an exciting yet challenging chapter in our human story. It's a journey filled with incredible possibilities but also with significant challenges. The key is to remember that AI is a tool. It doesn't have a will of its own. It reflects our intentions, our decisions, and our values. That leaves the future of AI in our human hands.

It's up to us to guide its development, to use it responsibly and ethically, and to ensure all share its benefits. Humans can and will define how this chapter in our story unfolds. Let's take a deeper dive into the organizational implications of AI usage and discuss ways the workforce can prepare for the changes brought on by the disruption and ethical challenges of AI.

Embracing Technological Disruption: AI and Organizational Growth

In a world that is continuously evolving and transforming, the mantra for survival is adaptability. The rise of artificial intelligence represents a monumental shift in our technological landscape, which is a disruption both daunting and tremendously potent. Here, we'll explore how organizations can embrace this technological disruption, leveraging AI as a catalyst for growth and profitability. AI has fundamentally altered the business landscape across all industries and sectors. Its influence is transforming business models, driving efficiency, and fostering innovation. This transformation heralds a new era where data and algorithms become the new engines of growth.

One tangible example of AI-driven disruption is in customer service. Traditional, human-driven customer service models are being increasingly supplemented or even replaced by AI-powered chatbots and virtual assistants. These tools not only streamline customer service but also enhance customer engagement by providing personalized, round-the-clock support. As businesses embrace this transformation, they unlock new dimensions of customer relationship management, fostering customer loyalty and improving brand value.

The power of AI extends far beyond customer service. In supply chain management, AI algorithms can predict demand, optimize logistics, and manage inventories, driving efficiency and cost-effectiveness. In marketing applications, AI tools provide insights into customer behavior, enabling targeted and personalized marketing campaigns. In human resources, AI systems streamline recruitment, talent management, and employee engagement. AI's influence permeates every facet of an organization, driving growth and fostering a culture of innovation.

However, we need to recognize that managing AI's potential requires more than just technological prowess. Organizations must foster an AI-ready culture, one that embraces change, promotes learning, and encourages innovation. As AI systems become integral to organizational operations, leaders must ensure their teams have the requisite skills and mindset to engage with AI.

Crucially, this involves a shift in the perception of AI. Rather than viewing AI as a threat or a competitor, organizations must foster a view of AI as a collaborator, a tool that augments human potential. This involves promoting a culture of lifelong learning, where reskilling and upskilling become the norm rather than the exception.

For instance, employees whose roles involve routine tasks that AI can automate must be given opportunities to reskill and transition into roles that require uniquely human capabilities such as critical thinking, creativity, and emotional intelligence. On the other hand, employees in strategic roles must be upskilled to understand and leverage AI systems, ensuring that AI-driven insights are effectively integrated into decision-making processes.

At its core, the rise of AI necessitates a holistic transformation within organizations. Technological transformation must be complemented by cultural and structural changes. This includes developing robust data governance policies, ensuring ethical AI practices, and fostering a culture of transparency and accountability. Robust data governance policies will ensure data privacy, prevent data breaches, and uphold the trust of customers and employees. Additionally, AI systems must be developed and used ethically, ensuring fairness, preventing bias, and maintaining transparency.

Embracing AI also necessitates a rethinking of organizational structures. Traditional hierarchical structures may give way to more fluid, agile structures that promote collaboration, learning, and innovation. Leaders in an AI-driven organization are not just decision-makers but facilitators who empower their teams, promote a culture of learning, and drive innovation.

AI represents a disruption that organizations cannot afford to ignore. Change, after all, is inevitable. In the face of technological disruption, the choice is not whether to change but how to change. As we embrace AI and the change it brings, we are not just adapting to a new reality but shaping it, steering our organizations towards a future where human potential and AI converge to drive unprecedented growth and innovation.

The Ethical Dimensions of AI - Challenges and Considerations

To truly understand the nature of AI and its implications for the future, we must take time to examine the critical ethical dimensions of AI and the challenges organizations face as they embrace AI and the changes it brings. We must proactively address ethical considerations to ensure that AI technologies are deployed responsibly and for the greater benefit of society. By acknowledging the ethical challenges and implementing robust frameworks, organizations can take advantage of AI's potential while safeguarding against potential risks. While its benefits are profound and far-reaching, the ethical landscape accompanying this technology is often complex, and a measured, practical approach is necessary. Let's have a look at the ethics of AI.

A Look into AI's Ethical Quagmire

Understanding the ethical dimensions of AI goes beyond mere programming. It dives into the very nature of the decisions we want our algorithms to make and the underlying values those decisions should reflect. How we choose to use AI becomes the bridge between computational proficiency and moral discernment.

This leads to the **Bias Conundrum:** AI systems learn from data. If this data is imbued with historical biases, AI could inadvertently amplify them. For instance, if a hiring AI tool is trained on past hiring data from a company with unconscious gender bias, the tool might favor one gender over the other.

Accountability in the Age of AI

When AI-driven systems make decisions, the accountability conundrum emerges. Who is responsible when AI makes a mistake?

Is it the developers, the users, or the AI itself? At play here is **Transparent Decision Making:** It's essential for AI systems to be transparent. Decision-makers should understand how conclusions are derived. In sectors like healthcare, where AI might recommend treatment paths, clarity in decision-making processes is non-negotiable.

AI and Individual Privacy

With AI's capability to process vast amounts of data, concerns regarding individual privacy are paramount. While data is the lifeline of AI, striking a balance between personal privacy and data access is pivotal. We must provide for **Informed Consent:** Users should be informed about how their data is being utilized. Transparency in data collection, processing, and usage can pave the way for trust in AI-driven systems.

The Power Dynamics of AI

AI has the potential to be a great equalizer or a tool for further widening disparities. Who controls AI, the kind of data it's fed, and the decisions it makes can concentrate power in a few hands, leading to potential misuse.

One solution is **Decentralizing AI:** Making AI tools and training accessible to a broader audience can ensure a more balanced power dynamic. Open-source AI, community-driven projects, and transparent AI policies are steps in the right direction.

Ethical AI: A Guiding Framework

As organizations embed AI into their core, an ethical framework becomes indispensable. This should not merely be a static document but dynamic, evolving guidelines. These guidelines should outline:

Inclusive Design: Involve diverse teams in AI design and decision-making. Diversity can provide a myriad of perspectives, ensuring that AI is holistic and considers multiple viewpoints.

Continuous Review: Ethical considerations aren't a one-time activity. Regular reviews and feedback loops can help refine AI tools, making them more aligned with ethical norms.

Stakeholder Engagement: Engage with consumers, employees, and stakeholders. Their feedback can offer invaluable insights into AI's real-world implications, ensuring the technology remains grounded and beneficial.

Safeguarding the Future

As AI continues to be an increasingly larger presence, placing ethics at the heart of development and deployment can ensure a harmonious coexistence between humans and technology. Consider these ethical safeguards:

Ethics Training for AI Professionals: Equip those at the forefront of AI development with the tools and knowledge to weave ethical considerations into their creations. Workshops, seminars, and collaborative platforms can serve as vital touchpoints.

Public Discourse and Awareness: Engage the public in discussions about AI ethics. Their insights, concerns, and aspirations can help shape a future where AI serves all of humanity, not just a select few.

Upskilling and Reskilling in the AI Era: Preparing the Workforce for Change

Amidst the constant hum of technological advancements, AI stands out as a groundbreaking force, revolutionizing industries and dictating new norms. But, while we revel in its potential, we must acknowledge the parallel narrative—a significant shift in the skills required for the jobs of today and tomorrow.

Embracing AI means preparing ourselves and our workforce for this change, which we can do through the power of upskilling and reskilling.

Why Upskilling and Reskilling Matter

Before we examine the 'how,' let's first understand the 'why.' The AI-driven paradigm isn't merely about machines replacing humans; it's about machines augmenting human capabilities. This augmentation necessitates new skills and the ability to learn continuously.

Enter the *Redundancy Dilemma*. With AI automating repetitive tasks, many traditional roles risk redundancy. However, this doesn't spell a jobless future but instead emphasizes a shift in the nature of jobs available. Herein lies the significance of upskilling, keeping one's skill set relevant and competitive.

Differentiating Upskilling and Reskilling

In our quest to understand and adapt to AI, it's crucial to distinguish between upskilling and reskilling:

Upskilling: It's about expanding on your current skill set. For instance, a software developer might upskill by learning about AI programming paradigms.

Reskilling: This is more transformative, where individuals acquire a new set of skills to transition into a different role. A bank teller, for instance, might reskill to become a customer relations specialist in an era of AI-powered kiosks. Remember that these aren't just business buzzwords or abstract concepts. They are very real and very personal journeys that countless individuals undertake in the pursuit of staying relevant in the current AI-dominated age. To truly grasp the power of these processes, sometimes it's best to witness them in action through the lens of a real-life tale. Let me share with you an inspiring story that perfectly encapsulates everything we've discussed so far. Meet Elena, an individual whose digital transformation is a testament to the essence of upskilling and adapting. Elena's story is not just about changing one's professional path; it's about embracing change, leaning into uncertainty, and, above all, the relentless pursuit of growth.

Elena's Digital Reinvention

Meet Elena, a dedicated customer service representative at a renowned bank. For over 15 years, she mastered the art of communication, handling customer queries with grace and empathy. Elena was the embodiment of the bank's values, beloved by both colleagues and customers. With the integration of AI-driven chatbots, the bank aimed to streamline basic queries, offering 24/7 assistance to its clientele. The initial reaction was mixed. Many feared that these chatbots would replace the human touch that Elena and her colleagues brought to the table. However, Elena, always having a knack for understanding customer behavior, saw an opportunity. She volunteered to be part of a team liaising between the tech experts and customer service reps. Her goal? To refine the chatbot's responses to be more empathetic and customer-centric. She not only provided real-life examples of complex queries but also shed light on the nuances of human emotions, helping the AI learn and adapt. Her feedback was invaluable in creating a chatbot that mirrored the bank's ethos. But Elena didn't stop there. She took courses on AI fundamentals, understanding the mechanisms behind these chatbots. Soon, she was not just a customer service representative but a critical connection, ensuring the seamless integration of AI into customer service, combining efficiency with empathy. Elena's story highlights a profound truth. AI and automation, while powerful, require the human touch to realize their full potential. By understanding and aligning with technological advancements, one can not only remain relevant but also ascend to roles of greater significance and impact.

Strategies for Effective Upskilling and Reskilling

Now that we've set the stage, let's dive into the strategies:

1. Identifying Skill Gaps: Start with a robust skills audit. Understand the current skills landscape within your organization and compare this against the needs of the future. Engage with industry experts, tap into market research, and use AI-powered analytics tools for a comprehensive analysis.

2. Cultivating a Learning Culture: Foster an organizational ethos that celebrates continuous learning. This isn't just about offering training programs but about creating an environment where learning is integral.

3. Personalized Learning Pathways: One size doesn't fit all. Utilize AI-driven platforms that curate personalized learning paths for individuals, ensuring higher engagement and retention.

4. Collaborative Learning Platforms: Harness the collective intelligence of your workforce. Create platforms where peers can teach and learn from each other. Platforms like internal wikis, forums, and seminars can facilitate this.

5. Industry-Academia Partnerships: Engage with educational institutions. Their research and fresh perspectives, combined with your industry insights, can create curricula that are both cutting-edge and relevant.

6. Focus on Soft Skills: While technical prowess is essential, soft skills like critical thinking, empathy, and adaptability become equally crucial in the AI era. These skills empower individuals to manage the nuances of AI-augmented roles effectively. Leaders need to play a pivotal role in this transition. By actively participating in upskilling and reskilling initiatives, they send a strong message about its importance. All learning comes with mistakes, and leaders should foster environments where mistakes are seen as learning opportunities.

While the path of upskilling and reskilling is laden with promise, it isn't devoid of challenges. Change is often met with resistance. Transparent communication about the 'why' behind these initiatives can mitigate this. And while initial enthusiasm is common, sustained engagement can wane. Gamified learning platforms, rewards, and recognition can keep the momentum going.

The Broader Ecosystem: Going Beyond the Organization

Preparing the workforce for the AI era is more than just an organizational responsibility. It's a collective endeavor. Governments can play a pivotal role by framing policies encouraging upskilling and reskilling. Subsidies, tax breaks, and public awareness campaigns can be instrumental. Community-driven learning hubs can democratize access to knowledge, ensuring that no one is left behind in this transition. As we've been emphasizing the importance of strategies for effective upskilling and reskilling, it might be illuminating to shift our gaze from the theoretical to the practical, grounding our understanding in the tangible. We often learn best when we see theory come alive, when abstract principles manifest in the real world, guiding actual decisions and outcomes. With that in mind, let's turn our attention to an enterprise that didn't just acknowledge the importance of upskilling but took all the necessary steps to make it a reality.

Let me introduce you to AT&T's initiative—a remarkable testament to the power and significance of preparing a workforce for the future. This case will not only substantiate the strategies we've discussed but also inspire leaders to recognize the potential of a proactive approach.

Case Study: AT&T's $1 Billion Upskilling Initiative

Let's examine another case study, this one of communications giant AT&T, and how they took the need for upskilling and reskilling and transformed an entire workforce.

Background: Around 2013, AT&T, one of the world's largest telecommunications companies, was at a crossroads. The technological landscape was evolving rapidly, and AT&T realized that a significant portion of its 250,000 employees lacked the necessary skills to keep up with the company's shift from hardware to the cloud.

The Initiative: Instead of opting for large-scale layoffs, AT&T set out on a massive, multi-million-dollar initiative called "Future Ready". This ambitious endeavor aimed to upskill its existing workforce to meet the demands of the new technological era.

They did this with:

- **Personalized Learning Paths:** Employees were offered a self-service platform where they could see the roles the company needed to fill in the future, understand the skills those roles required, and then take online courses tailored to those roles.
- **Collaboration with Educational Institutions:** AT&T didn't go about this massive undertaking alone. They partnered with online platforms like Coursera and Udacity, and even traditional institutions like Georgia Tech, to curate specialized courses.
- **Focus on Soft Skills:** Recognizing the importance of adaptability and critical thinking, AT&T provided leadership training to 130,000 employees to foster these invaluable soft skills.
- **Clear Communication:** The initiative's success was partly due to the company's clear communication. Employees knew what was at stake. As Randall Stephenson, AT&T's CEO at the time, candidly put it, "There is a need to retool yourself, and you should not expect to stop."

Outcome: By 2020, AT&T had successfully reskilled over half of its workforce, a feat that not only safeguarded the company's future but also the careers of thousands of its employees.

Key Takeaways

AT&T's journey underscores several significant lessons. First, a proactive approach to upskilling and reskilling is far more productive and cost-effective than reactive measures. Secondly, collaborations with external institutions can amplify the quality and reach of learning initiatives. Lastly, transparent communication is crucial in driving engagement and commitment from employees. With our exploration into AT&T's approach towards upskilling and reskilling, it becomes clear that organizational change is just one facet of the AI-driven transformation. The leadership spearheading these initiatives is crucial. It's not merely about policies and training programs; it's also about vision, foresight, and the courage to venture into the uncharted. Drawing from this understanding, let's move on from telecommunications giants like AT&T to the corridors of Silicon Valley. There, at the heart of innovation, another compelling story unfolds—that of Sundar Pichai, the strategic mind steering Google into the AI era. This case study epitomizes how individual leadership can shape, influence, and drive technological transformation at a grand scale.

Case Study: Sundar Pichai and Google's AI Odyssey

The Visionary at the Helm: Sundar Pichai, an engineer by training and a visionary by nature, took the reins of Google in 2015. Under his leadership, Google, already a tech behemoth, began its transformation from a search-centric company to an AI-first enterprise. Pichai's vision was clear: to make Google's products more useful and relevant in an AI-driven world.

The AI-First Shift: Pichai's leadership marked a distinct shift in Google's approach. He recognized that the next wave of computing was not just about connecting people to information but about making that connection seamless, intuitive, and personalized. This vision led to the integration of AI into every facet of Google's products, from search to advertising, from cloud computing to hardware. For instance, Google Photos, under Pichai's guidance, began using AI to automatically categorize and tag photos, making it easier for users to find and organize their memories. Google Assistant, the company's virtual assistant, became more conversational and context-aware, thanks to deep learning algorithms.

Championing Open AI: Pichai was not just focused on leveraging AI for Google's products. He believed in the democratization of AI. Under his leadership, Google opened up its machine learning framework, TensorFlow, to the public. This move allowed developers worldwide to build on Google's advanced machine learning tools, fostering innovation and ensuring that the benefits of AI were accessible to all.

Ethical AI: A Pillar of Leadership: Pichai's leadership in the AI field was not without its challenges. As AI's influence grew, so did concerns about its ethical implications. Recognizing this, Pichai championed the cause of responsible AI. In 2018, he unveiled Google's AI Principles, a set of guidelines that committed the company to building AI that was socially beneficial, fair, accountable, and safe.

These principles also outlined areas where Google would not deploy AI, such as in weapons or technologies that could harm humanity. This commitment to ethical AI underscored Pichai's belief that technology should serve humanity, not the other way around.

Fostering a Culture of Continuous Learning: Pichai's vision for an AI-first Google also meant preparing its workforce for the AI era. He championed initiatives that fostered a culture of continuous learning within Google. Employees were encouraged to upskill, with access to courses on machine learning, data science, and other AI-related domains. This focus on learning ensured that Google's workforce was not just equipped to handle the challenges of the present but was also prepared for the innovations of the future.

A Legacy of Transformation: Sundar Pichai's leadership at Google is a testament to the transformative power of vision, innovation, and ethical commitment. Under his guidance, Google has not only solidified its position as a leader in the AI space but has also set the gold standard for how companies should approach AI ethically and responsibly. This story serves as a beacon for leaders worldwide, illuminating the path to harnessing AI's potential while staying grounded in values, ethics, and a commitment to serving humanity. As we work deeper into the complexities of the AI era, Pichai's journey at Google offers invaluable insights into the confluence of leadership, innovation, and responsibility.

Exercise: AI Integration and Future Planning

It's time for this chapter's exercise, and it's meant to help professionals visualize and strategically plan for the role of AI in their current job roles and industries.

Step 1: Personal Job Role Analysis

A) List down your primary job responsibilities. For instance, if you're in marketing, your tasks might include content creation, data analysis, customer outreach, etc.

B) Next to each responsibility, mark whether you believe AI could play a role. Could an AI tool assist with content optimization? Might machine learning enhance data analysis?

Step 2: AI Exploration

A) Research AI advancements related to your profession. Use platforms like Google Scholar, industry blogs, or even YouTube for insights on how AI is reshaping your profession.

B) Document potential AI tools or software that could augment or transform tasks from your list.

Step 3: Upskilling and Reskilling

A) Identify areas in your job role where human skills will always be indispensable. For instance, in our previous marketing example, while AI might help optimize content, creativity and human connection in content creation are irreplaceable.

B) List down new skills or training you might need to contend with the AI-integrated future of your job. If data analysis in marketing is enhanced by machine learning, perhaps a course in understanding machine learning for marketing would be beneficial.

Step 4: Reflect and Discuss

A) Consider how your role might evolve in an AI-integrated workspace. Are there areas where you can take the lead in integrating AI? Can you be the bridge, much like Elena in our anecdote?

B) If possible, discuss your findings and reflections with a mentor or colleague. Gain insights from their perspectives and understand how they view the convergence of AI in your shared industry.

With this exercise, and with all you've learned within this chapter, you and your organization can be prepared for the future of AI, including its challenges, ethical considerations, and the need for continuous learning to ensure you make the most of AI's potential.

Key Takeaways

- AI is not just a technological tool; it's transforming our societal fabric and how we function in our workplaces. Its integration is inevitable and far-reaching.
- While AI promises efficiency and innovation, the true value lies in a balanced blend of human intuition and AI's capabilities. Organizational growth with AI doesn't replace but rather augments human roles.
- As with all powerful tools, AI carries ethical implications. From bias in algorithms to data privacy, we must handle these challenges conscientiously, ensuring AI benefits all without compromising values.
- Change can be daunting, especially when it threatens our

professional roles. Yet, the focus should be on upskilling and reskilling. The AI era doesn't render us obsolete; it offers a chance to evolve, much like Elena did in her digital odyssey. Prepare, adapt, and soar.

CHAPTER 7

Embracing Change

In this chapter, we'll dive deep into the art of embracing change. It begins by nurturing an adaptive mindset—a foundational key in this ever-evolving world. We're not just talking about fleeting adjustments; it's about fundamentally reconfiguring our mindset to be fluid, open, and always ready to learn. Embracing change doesn't come without its challenges. That's why building resilience is so important. It's like building muscles; the more we face and handle challenges with confidence, the stronger and more resilient we become.

To help you build resilience and remain prepared to handle all the changes this life can bring, we'll use this chapter to explore a toolkit of techniques designed to help us engage with change more effectively. From time-tested strategies to novel methodologies, these tools will become your go-to resources as you move ahead.

We'll conclude this chapter with a shift from tools to thwart the turbulence of change to the serene practice of mindfulness. This isn't just a buzzword; mindfulness is a powerful way to anchor yourself when change stirs things up. We'll use a trusted exercise to learn how to stay present, calm, and centered, no matter the external shifts. Let's get started.

Developing an Open and Adaptive Mindset

Life's unpredictable nature demands that we be swift. At the intersection of change, we're handed a choice—to resist or to embrace. While the former seems instinctual, the latter, though daunting, equips us with a growth-centric mindset, essential in our world that's in perpetual flux. This chapter is about more than merely accepting change; it's a celebration of the opportunity to grow.

The Value of Openness

Openness is more than just a virtue; it's a necessity. Openness isn't just about acceptance; it's about anticipation. And that is the anticipation of possibilities that come from change, understanding that not all change is a threat. Sometimes, it's an invitation. This extends beyond personal open-mindedness into the professional world.

Exercises like feedforward (the opposite of feedback) bring diverse voices to the table to talk about the future. Such conversations bring about innovation and engender progress. An open mindset prioritizes the collective over the individual. Instead of solitary achievements, the focus shifts towards shared milestones, creating an environment where the sum is indeed greater than its parts.

The Science Behind an Open Mind

Neuroplasticity: a term that reveals our brain's extraordinary adaptability. This scientific concept emphasizes our mind's malleability, affirming that it isn't a fixed entity but one that's capable of great change. Challenge and nurture it, and it rewards us with growth. Modern-day stressors, like the influx of information or encroaching deadlines, can be reframed as growth stimulants, pushing our cognitive boundaries.

But caution is key. We must remain vigilant to signs of overwhelm, like sleep disturbances or a drop in motivation, and adjust accordingly. The brain always tells us exactly what it needs, but we have to pause and listen.

Breaking the Echo Chamber

In our globally connected era, it's ironic how one can feel trapped within an echo chamber, constantly reinforced by our own biases and beliefs. It's imperative to consciously step out, absorb diverse views, and let varied voices enrich our narratives. Engage in challenging discussions, explore unfamiliar territories, and embrace divergent thinkers.

It's in this melting pot of ideas that brilliance emerges. Often, organizations and individuals surround themselves with 'yes-men.' However, it's the contrarian voices, the ones that challenge the status quo, that often drive breakthroughs. Inviting and, more importantly, listening to differing opinions and diverse voices can lead to unparalleled growth. An open and adaptive mindset isn't just cognitive gymnastics. It's an emotional journey, a social endeavor, and a graceful balancing of life's ebb and flow.

As we make our way through this world, brimming with uncertainties and opportunities alike, an open and adaptive mindset is a tremendous tool for making connections, discovering new ideas and perspectives, exercising empathy, and creating a foundation of sustained personal and professional growth. Every challenge is an invitation to learn, adapt, and flourish.

Managing Challenges with Confidence through Resilience Building

Resilience. It's a word we've all heard, perhaps even casually thrown around in conversations or team meetings. But truly grasping its depth, understanding its layers, and recognizing its undeniable power in our lives takes a little more reflection and intent. The truth is that we've all faced challenges, setbacks, and unexpected plot twists. Some are minor hiccups that we quickly brush off, while others, well, they knock the wind right out of us. Those are the moments when resilience isn't just a fancy word; it becomes a lifeline. So, what exactly is resilience? It's our ability to adapt, recover, and grow stronger from adversities. Some people are born with innate resilience, and for others, it's a learned skill.

Resilience can be cultivated, trained, and sharpened over time. And like any skill, it becomes more robust with every challenge we face. Resilience also goes hand-in-hand with confidence. The more you engage your resiliency skills, the more confident you will become in managing change.

Empathy and Emotional Intelligence -Their Roles in Resilience

Have you heard the phrase, "No man is an island?" We live in a world filled with other people, teeming with their aspirations, fears, and emotions. Recognizing and understanding these emotions in ourselves and others is what we term 'empathy,' and it's another essential tool in our resilience toolkit. Why? Because by being empathetic, we not only forge deeper connections with others but also better understand our own emotional mindset. This recognition equips us to anticipate, react to, and recover from setbacks in constructive ways. Building on empathy is the broader spectrum of emotional intelligence. This is your ability to recognize, understand, and manage emotions while also being attuned to the emotions of others. Having high emotional intelligence means you're better equipped to handle stressors and manage change.

Cognitive Flexibility: The Art of Mental Agility

Life is unpredictable. The only thing certain is its uncertainty. Here's where cognitive flexibility or mental agility comes into play. It's your brain's ability to swiftly switch between ideas or tasks and adapt to new situations, even when they don't go as planned. A rigid mindset can be likened to driving a car with flat tires – it's possible, but it's arduous and ineffective. Mental agility, on the other hand, ensures your tires are always pumped, ready to take on any terrain.

Adapting with Grace: Drawing from Dweck's Revolutionary Perspective

Dr. Carol Dweck's groundbreaking work on fixed and growth mindsets is vital to any discussion of resilience. She postulates that individuals with a fixed mindset believe their abilities are static and unchangeable. In contrast, those with a growth mindset believe that abilities can be developed. Consider James, a middle manager at a tech firm. Faced with a monumental project failure, he could easily drown in self-pity, believing he's just not "cut out" for success. But, recalling Dweck's perspective, he chose to see it as a lesson, a stepping stone. He embraced the growth mindset, believing in his potential to learn and improve. This perspective shift didn't just help him bounce back but carried him even farther in his career. Resilience isn't about avoiding falls. It's about rising every single time, learning, adapting, and growing. As you journey through life's ups and downs, remember that every challenge is an opportunity, every setback a lesson, and every adversity a chance to bolster resilience. The key is to think with confidence, lean into empathy, exercise your emotional intelligence, and let mental agility be your guide. And remember that every stumble, every obstacle, every "failure" is just a stepping stone, moving you closer to your goals, dreams, and aspirations. Working through change is not solely about adopting new strategies or techniques. More often, it boils down to inner strength —our resilience.

Think about the most challenging situations in your professional journey. Those times when information overload was at its peak, when deadlines loomed like dark clouds, and the balancing act between career and family felt like walking a tightrope. In those moments, did you not wish for a tad more resilience? For a mindset that could not only withstand such stressors but thrive amidst them? This brings us to a prime exemplar of resilience, someone who, beyond the boardrooms and corporate corridors, has showcased what it truly means to overcome challenges with sheer confidence. Let's turn our attention to the world of sports, where the lines between victory and defeat are starkly drawn. Consider Serena Williams. Her journey isn't just about tennis; it's about persistence, adaptability, and unwavering self-belief. As we dissect her story, let's extract lessons that aren't limited to the court's boundaries but resonate with the essence of our topic: embracing change with resilience.

Case Study: Serena Williams and the Embrace of Growth Mindset

When we look at the sports arena, there are a few names that resonate louder than the rest, and Serena Williams stands tall among them. However, let's take a moment to understand her trajectory not just as a sports genius but as a masterclass in Carol Dweck's principles of the growth mindset.

Humble Beginnings and Mindset Challenges: Serena, as a fledgling player, undeniably showcased remarkable talent. But talent, though a gift, comes with its own baggage. The weight of expectations, the glare of the spotlight, and the stifling notion of pre-ordained greatness can be challenging. There were times when Serena teetered on the brink, succumbing to pressure and responding to setbacks in ways that hinted at a fixed mindset. At moments like these, many might've thought, "Perhaps this is as far as she goes."

The Turning Point: Growth Mindset: Serena's story didn't end there; it merely pivoted. What's fascinating is her transition phase, where instead of lamenting losses as conclusive judgments of her capabilities, she began to interpret them as detours, not roadblocks. After a less-than-stellar match or when faced with vocal critics,

Serena's response became one of action: more hours honing her skills, recalibrating her strategies, and reinforcing her mental and emotional fortitude.

Growth in Action: This evolution in her approach rendered some palpable outcomes:

- **Epic Turnarounds:** Serena's matches turned into narratives of resilience. Even in situations where the odds were stacked against her, she orchestrated some of the most thrilling comebacks.
- **Tactical Evolution:** Tennis, like all sports, evolves. Fresh faces with new strategies emerged, but Serena was never one to be left behind. She adapted, she grew, and she continued her reign.

- **Battling Personal Storms**: Life threw curveballs, from injuries to deeply personal challenges and even the trials of motherhood. But armed with a growth mindset, Serena emerged each time, not just unbroken but stronger.

The Lens of Dweck's Wisdom: Drawing parallels with Carol Dweck's insights, Serena's persistence throughout her incredible career is a powerful testament to the idea that it isn't sheer talent alone that carves greatness. A growth mindset, underscored by perseverance and the belief in one's ability to evolve, makes all the difference. Serena Williams' career arc, intertwined with Dweck's principles, offers us a profound lesson. It's not the starting line that matters the most; it's the journey, including growth, evolution, and the undying spirit to move forward.

Embracing Change as a Continuous Process

As quickly as the world evolves, one thing remains undeniable: Change is inevitable. But here's the crux—it's not the occurrence of change that shapes our lives, but rather our response to it. Imagine, for a moment, standing by the shoreline, watching the waves approach. Some waves gently lap at our feet, while others might sweep us off into the unknown. Isn't this a beautiful metaphor for life's unpredictable nature? But why do some people seem to glide effortlessly through these waves while others struggle, getting caught in the undertow? It's not mere luck or chance; it's a conscious recognition of change as a continuous process and the ability to adapt to it gracefully.

Flowing with Life's Current
In our professional lives, we're often faced with situations that demand a reevaluation of strategies or approaches. For instance,

think about the rise of remote work or the significant shift towards digitalization in the last decade. Those who viewed these changes as threats or mere trends, unfortunately, found themselves floundering. On the other hand, individuals and organizations that saw these as opportunities to evolve and adapt prospered. This disparity stems from one's ability (or lack thereof) to see change as a current. Instead of fighting against it, why not go with the flow and see where it takes you?

Recognizing the Nuances

Let's be honest; not all changes feel great. Some are challenging and can be downright daunting. The sudden onset of a global pandemic, personal upheavals, or even rapid market shifts are testimonies to this fact. But remember, it's in these very moments of adversity that the seeds of growth are planted.

Consistent Growth Through Continuous Learning

The world doesn't pause; it continually moves, evolves, and transforms. To keep pace, it's imperative to foster a mindset of continuous learning. Equip yourself with new skills, knowledge, and perspectives.

When you're constantly learning, you're not only staying relevant but also preparing for future changes, ensuring that when the next change comes, you're ready to face it with confidence. In fact, the very essence of embracing change lies in your ability to see it as a teacher. Every shift and every transition offers a lesson. As with any class, the more attentive and receptive the student, the more profound the learning.

The Silver Lining

In all this talk about change, let's not forget its beautiful by-product: Innovation. When we're open to change, when we embrace it wholeheartedly, we're also inadvertently fostering an environment ripe for innovation. New ideas flourish, creativity blossoms, and before you know it, you're not just adapting to change; you're spearheading it. No, change isn't a sporadic event to brace for. It's a continuous, lifelong process. Instead of viewing it as a disruptive force, see it as an opportunity—an opportunity to grow, evolve, and, most importantly, become the best version of yourself.

The Future is Dynamic

Change is about movement and adaptability. As we stand at the brink of a future marked by unprecedented technological advancements, societal shifts, and evolving personal and professional landscapes, the ability to embrace change as a continuous process will be crucial.

Considering the theme of "Embracing Change as a Continuous Process," a compelling case study would be the transformational journey of Netflix. This company's narrative beautifully encapsulates how change can lead to remarkable success.

Think about when you're winding down after a long day, choosing the perfect show or movie to stream. Have you ever wondered about the behind-the-scenes evolution of the platform you're using? Enter Netflix. Their journey is a masterclass in embracing change, not as a one-time event but as a perpetual unfolding process. But before you think of Netflix as just another tech company, remember that its core strength lies in its adaptability, passion, and unwavering vision.

As we examine Netflix's story, you'll find it's not merely about entertainment; it's a testament to what organizations can achieve when they truly understand and apply the principles of continuous change.

Case Study: Netflix - Pioneering Change in Entertainment

Back in the late 90s, if someone had mentioned Netflix, it would have conjured images of red envelopes containing DVDs arriving in mailboxes. Founded in 1997, Netflix began as a service offering DVD rentals by mail. At this time, Blockbuster was the dominant player in the video rental industry. Few could have foreseen how Netflix would not only rival this behemoth but eventually lead to its decline.

Adapting to the Digital Revolution: By the mid-2000s, with the rise of faster internet connections, the concept of streaming media was beginning to take hold. Netflix, sensing this shift, launched its streaming service in 2007. Instead of clinging to their DVD-by-mail model, they recognized the potential of this new format. Their foresight was impeccable; streaming exploded in popularity while DVD rentals began their gradual decline.

This move was groundbreaking. While maintaining its DVD rental service, Netflix poured resources and focus into refining and expanding its streaming offering. They anticipated the change, adapted, and, as a result, began their ascent as a global streaming powerhouse.

Innovating Content Creation: But Netflix didn't stop there. Recognizing that merely hosting content wouldn't be enough in the long run, they ventured into content creation. In 2013, they released *House of Cards*, their first original series.

It was a gamble, but the show's success set the stage for a slew of original content, further cementing Netflix's dominance in the streaming world.

This move highlighted an essential lesson: Embracing change isn't just about adapting; it's about innovating and setting trends.

Facing Challenges Head-On: Like all organizations, Netflix faced challenges. With the rise of competitors like Amazon Prime, Disney+, and Apple TV+, the streaming landscape has become increasingly crowded. But Netflix's continuous commitment to change, evident in their investment in diverse content, global expansion, and technological improvements, has kept them at the forefront.

Lessons from Netflix's Journey: What can Netflix's ability to grapple with change teach us?

- **Anticipate Trends:** Netflix's early pivot to streaming demonstrated the power of foresight.
- **Innovate, Don't Just Adapt:** Moving into original content wasn't just an adaptation; it was a groundbreaking shift.
- **Stay Agile:** Despite its size, Netflix remains nimble, continuously tweaking its strategies based on viewer data and global trends.

Tools and Techniques for Embracing Change Effectively

We've spent a lot of time talking about managing and working through change, but what are the concrete tools and techniques that can guide us during the process?

1. **Dynamic SWOT Analysis** - Traditional SWOT (Strengths, Weaknesses, Opportunities, Threats) is often static. But in a rapidly evolving landscape, being dynamic is essential.

By continually updating and revising our SWOT analysis, we remain attuned to shifts in our environment.

2. **Mind Mapping** - This isn't just about scribbling thoughts on a canvas. It's an avenue for crystallizing ideas and establishing connections. By using platforms like 'MindMeister' or the age-old chart paper approach, we're not just brainstorming; we're laying down pathways for structured thinking.

3. **The Eisenhower Box** - This technique is simplicity personified. Stemming from Dwight Eisenhower's principles, it's a method I've employed to allocate tasks based on their urgency and significance. It's about discerning what truly demands your immediate attention.

4. **Scenario Planning Techniques** - Preempting the future, in many ways, feels like anticipating the next move in a game of chess. This isn't about mere prediction but rather preparation. By equipping ourselves with a multi-dimensional view, we become proactive, not just reactive.

5. **Digital Detoxes** - As counterintuitive as it may sound, especially in this era of constant connectivity, stepping away, even momentarily, from our screens can offer unparalleled clarity. It's not about isolation but introspection.

6. **Meditation & Mindfulness Apps** - Platforms like 'Headspace' and 'Calm' have been sanctuaries amidst the daily hustle. They are not merely apps; they're digital oases that offer moments of tranquility.

7. **Journaling** - The act of transferring thoughts to paper is therapeutic. It's more than a reflection; it's a heart-to-heart dialogue with oneself.

8. **Feedback Tools** - Platforms such as 'SurveyMonkey' act as mirrors, reflecting not just our strengths but also areas of growth.

9. **Emotional Intelligence Workshops** - EQ, as we know, is not just about understanding our own emotions but also those of others. It's the bridge that fosters connections and, more importantly, understanding.

10. **Resilience Training Programs** - Building resilience isn't a one-time endeavor. It's a continuous journey, and such programs have acted as my roadmap through any number of adversities.

Here are even more techniques that you can use when you need to offer and gather insights:

1. **Feedforward Mechanisms** - Going beyond the retrospective analysis of feedback, the technique of feedforward offers a proactive approach. This is about envisioning and acting on future possibilities. A feedforward mechanism in change management can channel efforts toward anticipated challenges and opportunities.

2. **Mentorship Circles** - Instead of the conventional one-on-one mentor-mentee dynamic, why not curate a circle? This would allow for a richer exchange of insights and experiences. Plus, much like how you'd prepare for meetings with mentors by setting goals, each member of the circle could set objectives, ensuring every interaction is both productive and enriching.

3. **Regenerative Breaks** - We all deal with periods of with stress. It's essential not just to disconnect but also to regenerate. This technique is about making time for regular disengagement, followed by activities that recharge the mind and soul. It isn't just a break; it's a renewal.

4. **Scenario-based Mindfulness** - Mindfulness isn't just about being present. It's about engaging with the present moment constructively. Through scenario-based exercises, one can harness mindfulness to anticipate, adapt, and act amidst change, ensuring we're not merely reactive but remarkably centered.

5. **The Reflect-Act-Transform (RAT) Model** - Reflect on current circumstances, act with precision, and continuously transform the approach. By adopting the RAT model, we integrate introspection, action, and evolution, fostering a more fluid response to change.

6. **The "What-If" Exploration** - Encourage sessions where teams indulge in "What-If" scenarios. It's not just about speculating but constructing potential solutions and pathways. It's a bit like playing chess, but with real-world consequences, preparing for multiple moves ahead.

7. **Holistic Health Checks** - Much like assessing the warning signals of excessive stress, like insomnia or dwindling motivation, organizations can institute regular "health checks" to gauge their adaptive capabilities, ensuring they're not just surviving change but truly thriving amidst it.

Incorporating these tools and techniques isn't just about managing change; it's about thriving amidst it. The real magic, however, doesn't lie in these tools but in our approach towards them. It's in our mindset, our openness, and the continuous pursuit of growth.

The Art of Iteration

Finally, let's remember that change isn't a one-off event. It's continuous. As you use these tools and techniques, keep refining them. Your SWOT analysis from last year might be different this year. The scenarios you planned for might have evolved. Iteration is key.

Keep fine-tuning your approach, ensuring you're not just responding to change but actively shaping it. By equipping ourselves effectively, we stand not just to survive change but truly thrive amidst it.

Exercise: "The Change Journey"

This exercise is designed to foster introspection, offer perspective, and propel actionable change. It's an invitation to dive deep into the nature of change, much like preparing for a strategic meeting – with intention, openness, and purpose.

1. Environment Setting:
Instead of the conventional, rigid workspace or study environment, choose a more relaxed setting. Perhaps a cozy corner in your home, a serene park, or a quiet café.

Remember how we discussed the importance of ambiance when meeting with a mentor? Let's replicate that. Atmosphere can be a catalyst for reflection.

2. Mapping the Change Landscape:
On a piece of paper, jot down the significant changes you've encountered over the past year. They can be professional, personal, or a mix of both.

3. Emotion Mapping:

Next to each change, pen down the initial emotion you felt. Was it apprehension, excitement, anxiety, or joy? Just as we understand our stressors and their impact on our resilience, understanding our emotional responses helps chart our change journey.

4. The Reflective Pause:

Take a moment here. Breathe deeply. Recall our emphasis on re-generative breaks and the essence of mindfulness. This pause is a momentary disconnection to dive within, to truly engage with each emotion and understand its roots.

5. The "What-If" Exploration:

For each change and corresponding emotion, write a "What if?" scenario. For instance, "What if I had embraced the change with more enthusiasm?" or "What if I had sought advice earlier?". This exercise, rooted in speculative yet constructive scenarios, allows us to visualize alternate pathways and outcomes.

6. Crafting the Forward Path:

Now, for each "What if?" scenario, draft a small action plan. Like setting goals for our mentor meetings, these mini-action plans are your roadmap for future change scenarios. It's about ensuring the next time a similar change occurs, you're even better equipped emotionally and practically.

7. Closing Reflection:

To wrap up, sit back and soak in the insights gained. Every change, every emotion, every "What if?" has unraveled a lesson. Recognize and appreciate these learnings. And remember, every change is a stepping stone to personal and professional evolution. Engaging in this exercise isn't merely about ticking off a task. It's a rendez-vous with oneself, a strategic interaction with the core of our be-ing. It's about understanding that change isn't just an external event; it's an internal journey. Embrace it with grace, intention, and positivity. After all, as we often remind ourselves, it's not the change but our approach to it that truly defines the outcome.

Key Takeaways

- To truly master the benefits of change, we must first grasp the dynamics that might hinder progress. This is how feed-forward functions, enabling participants to ignite positive conversations and amplify cooperative energy.
- In this ever-evolving landscape, maintaining an open and adaptive mindset is critical to growth. We need to understand the sheer value of openness, the groundbreaking views of experts like Dweck, and how to sidestep the stifling echo chambers.
- Challenges are inevitable, but how we tackle them—armed with confidence and resilience—defines our journey. Remember those typical stressors? They're not just hurdles but opportunities to demonstrate and hone our resilience.
- Rather than resisting change, why not go with the flow? Drawing from our experiences, whether structured formal meetings or informal chats in comfy corners, every encounter teaches us more about embracing change.
- Crafting a high-performance team or preparing meticulously for a strategic meeting all boils down to having the right tools and techniques. These aren't just for managing tasks, but life's myriad changes.
- Just as we wouldn't dive into a strategic session without prepping, why approach life any differently? Practicing mindfulness, especially in these changing times, offers unparalleled clarity.

- Every change, every pivot, every twist in our narrative brings with it lessons and opportunities. Embrace the change, and let it move you forward.

CHAPTER 8

Change and Resilience

A s we wind down our journey through the complexity of change, let's zoom in on one of the most potent elements that underpins our ability to thrive amidst constant shifts: resilience. We discussed resilience briefly in the last chapter when we explored how to best embrace change, but here, we're diving much deeper. In a world of information overload, deadline pressures, and constant accessibility, your ability to bounce back becomes more than just a personal quality; it becomes an organizational asset. Think of it as the connective tissue between change and long-term success. This final chapter is a robust toolbox tailored for professionals and leaders like you who face complicated, ever-changing landscapes. Here, we'll explore the nuanced relationship between change and resilience, providing actionable strategies to fortify not just emotional resilience but also mental and social resilience. You'll gain insights into flexibility and adaptability—skills vital to any high-performing team—and we'll discuss how to nurture networks that add to your social capital, making you not just resilient but also resourceful. By the end, you'll have the tools to not only confront change head-on but also to manage change with finesse and confidence. Get ready to construct your personal and professional resilience plan; this is where theory meets action, setting you on a path of sustainable growth and adaptability.

Understanding the Relationship Between Change and Resilience

It's crucial to understand that change and resilience are complementary forces—two sides of the same coin. If you remember our conversation about cooperation, synergy, and high-performance teams, the one thing that stood out was the importance of adaptable dynamics. Much like that, the relationship between change and resilience is a dynamic one, where one pushes and the other pulls until balance is found.

The Nature of Change and Resilience: A Symbiotic Relationship

While we often look at change as a disruptor, a force that pushes us out of our comfort zones, it's also a catalyst. Resilience is our response—a deeply ingrained mechanism that lets us bounce back, adapt, and thrive amidst adversity. Just as we discussed the importance of identifying key elements for creating high-performing teams, it's essential to understand that change and resilience can't exist without each other. Change pushes our boundaries, and resilience allows us to morph, mold, and fit into these new spaces without breaking.

The Complex Web of Biology: Behind Resilience and Stress Management

To make this more relatable, let's dive into a familiar topic—the physiological stressors we encounter. Remember when we spoke about the various stressors like information overload, deadline pressures, and constant accessibility? Here's where the story gets intriguing. The biology behind resilience and stress management is a complex web of interconnected systems, all working in tandem. At the heart of it, we have our brain, the epicenter of stress response. When we face stressors, our brain activates the "fight or flight" mechanism. The adrenal glands pump adrenaline, increasing our heart rate, pumping more blood to our muscles, and preparing us to either face the challenge (fight) or run away (flight). This immediate response, while useful in short spurts, can be detrimental when prolonged, leading to chronic stress symptoms like insomnia and lack of motivation.

Now, let's interject resilience into this scenario. Resilience isn't about preventing the fight or flight response; instead, it's about returning to a state of balance swiftly after the threat has passed. It involves another aspect of our biology—the parasympathetic nervous system, often called the "rest and digest" system. This system counteracts the effects of adrenaline, bringing our heart rate down, slowing our breathing, and allowing us to return to a calm state.

The more resilient we are, the faster and more efficiently this system kicks in after a stressor has been encountered. The delicate balance between these two systems showcases how our biology is primed for resilience. In essence, our body, much like our mind, is always seeking equilibrium, and resilience is its tool.

Why Resilience Matters: More than Just Bouncing Back

Beyond the biological imperative, resilience offers an abundance of advantages in our daily lives. It allows us to grapple with the uncertainties of our environment with a balanced approach. Reflecting on our previous discussions, we noted how encountering challenges and overcoming them leads to confidence and contentment.

This sentiment, in a nutshell, is the value of resilience. Resilience, however, is more than just bouncing back. It's about absorbing the essence of every challenge and every change and using it to foster personal growth. It equips us with the tools to not just survive in a continually changing environment but to thrive and flourish.

Embracing Resilience as a Lifelong Companion

Our journey through understanding the relationship between change and resilience brings us to a meaningful realization. Just as we'd never enter a challenging project without a well-thought-out action plan, navigating the complexities of life without resilience is a path fraught with unnecessary challenges.

We've seen the complexity of the biology that supports resilience. We've understood its value in making us more adept at handling the stressors we spoke of earlier. Most importantly, we've recognized that resilience isn't a static trait—it's a dynamic quality shaped by experiences, challenges, and our proactive efforts to nurture it.

In the upcoming sections, we'll go even deeper into specific aspects of resilience. We'll explore the emotional, mental, and social dimensions, ensuring that by the end of this chapter, you're well-equipped with a holistic understanding and actionable strategies to make resilience second nature.

Resilience in Action: Stephen Hawking's Odyssey

To many, Stephen Hawking is a symbol of boundless resilience and indomitable spirit. A Cambridge cosmologist of great promise, Hawking's world took a drastic turn when, at the age of 21, he was diagnosed with a rare early-onset, slow-progressing form of motor neuron disease called Amyotrophic Lateral Sclerosis (ALS), also known as Lou Gehrig's disease, which resulted in his gradual paralysis over the decades.

The Crushing Diagnosis: Hawking's initial prognosis was grim. Doctors gave him a life expectancy of just two years. The emotional toll was immense. In his own words, "I felt it was very unfair—why should this happen to me? At the time, I thought my life was over and that I would never realize the potential I felt I had."

The Spark of Resilience: However, rather than succumbing to despair, a significant incident provided a fresh perspective. While in the hospital, he encountered a boy dying of leukemia. Compared to that boy's suffering, Hawking felt his own situation seemed more bearable. It was this relative perspective that propelled him to not only continue his academic pursuits but to elevate them.

Achievements Against All Odds: Defying all medical odds, not only did he live until the age of 76, but he also made groundbreaking contributions to the field of theoretical physics. His book, *A Brief History of Time*, became an international bestseller, making complex scientific concepts accessible to the general public.

Despite being reliant on a wheelchair and eventually losing his ability to speak, he utilized a speech-generating device, operated via a cheek muscle, to communicate. This allowed him to deliver lectures, write books, and engage in debates.

A Legacy of Resilience: Stephen Hawking's resilience is a testament to the power of the human spirit. He once remarked, "My expectations were reduced to zero when I was 21. Everything since then has been a bonus." Despite facing monumental physical challenges, he not only thrived in his professional endeavors but also led a life full of humor, adventure, and curiosity.

Hawking's journey illustrates that resilience is more than just the ability to bounce back from adversity. It's about transforming challenges into springboards for greatness. As we reflect upon his life, we're reminded that our potential is not defined by our circumstances but by our response to them.

When we examine the archives of human achievement and exploration, we can't help but marvel at the sheer resilience and indefatigable spirit of individuals like Stephen Hawking. His odyssey, riddled with challenges both physical and intellectual, reminds us that the boundaries we often perceive are, in essence, self-imposed limitations. But as we're inspired by Hawking's journey through the cosmos and the mysteries of black holes, it becomes even more imperative to explore the profound layers of human experience and psyche. Enter Viktor Frankl's quest for meaning. From the tangible sphere of quantum physics to the ethereal dimensions of the human soul, Frankl's pilgrimage through the harrowing landscapes of concentration camps in search of purpose provides an arresting juxtaposition. It's a testament that, whether amidst the vastness of the universe or the inner confines of the human mind, resilience is our most profound wayfinder, guiding us toward purpose and understanding.

Let's examine Frankl's introspective insights, illuminating the essence of resilience in the face of unimaginable adversity.

The Triumph of the Spirit: Viktor Frankl's Quest for Meaning

Viktor Frankl, a neurologist, psychiatrist, and Holocaust survivor, is a prime example of a human being's capacity to handle profound adversity with unparalleled resilience. His experiences during the Holocaust shaped his therapeutic approach, culminating in the development of logotherapy, which emphasizes the human search for meaning.

The Abyss of the Concentration Camps: During World War II, Frankl, along with his family, was deported to Nazi concentration camps. Over the span of three years, he was transferred between various camps, including Auschwitz. Tragically, apart from his sister, all of his family members, including his wife, perished in the camps. Throughout this horrifying ordeal, Frankl made a crucial observation: Those who could hold onto a sense of purpose or meaning in life, no matter how small, were more resilient to the relentless suffering and more likely to survive.

Birth of Logotherapy: Emerging from the Holocaust, Frankl penned the book Man's Search for Meaning, recounting his experiences and observations in the camps. He highlighted that even in the most dehumanizing circumstances, individuals could find a sense of purpose. Frankl himself found meaning in the thought of reuniting with his family and in his desire to write his book. This perspective didn't negate suffering but helped him maneuver through it. Frankl's therapeutic approach, logotherapy, is founded on the premise that the primary human drive is not pleasure, as Freud suggested, but the pursuit of what we find meaningful. When individuals face an existential vacuum or a lack of meaning, they become susceptible to despair and other mental health challenges.

Legacy Beyond the Holocaust: Post-war, Frankl returned to Vienna and played a significant role in reconstructing the city's neurological department. He authored 39 books, which have been translated into numerous languages. Moreover, his teachings on logotherapy continue to influence therapeutic approaches worldwide. His journey teaches us an invaluable lesson: When confronted with extreme adversity, it's not the circumstances we're thrown into but the choices we make in response to those circumstances that define our experiences. As Frankl himself stated, "Everything can be taken from a man but one thing: the last of the human freedoms—to choose one's attitude in any given set of circumstances, to choose one's own way."

Cultivating Resilience in Modern Times

Transitioning from the intense narratives of historical conflicts, let's shift our focus to the pressing challenges of today's world. As we navigate through an era marked by complex global issues, with climate crises looming and technological advancements like AI reshaping our lives, it's tempting to think our struggles are unique compared to those of the past. Yet, despite our battles bearing new faces – wars, political upheavals, economic challenges like inflation, energy crises, and soaring debt – the fundamental need for resilience remains the same. We confront obstacles that test our endurance, our values, and our ability to adapt. In this fast-evolving, interconnected global landscape, stressors arise not only from immediate, discernible threats but also from the broader implications of these crises. The ever-present strain of geopolitical tensions, the uncertainties of fluctuating economies, and the relentless pace of technological change all underscore that our era is fraught with its own set of trials. The key, as illustrated by historical resilience, lies not in the nature of these challenges but in our response to them. Just as individuals have faced and overcome monumental crises in the past, we too are equipped with choices in how we interpret and respond to our contemporary challenges. Is a demanding job amid economic instability a source of stress, or an opportunity for innovation and personal growth? Do global issues like climate change immobilize us, or motivate us to take action and find solutions? Indeed, while the context and scale of challenges evolve, the underlying qualities of adaptability, purpose, and perspective remain crucial. In a time when change is constant and the future uncertain, the commitment to self-awareness and resilience is more critical than ever. It's about understanding that the complexities of today's world call for an enhanced approach to resilience, one that integrates lessons from the past with the realities of the present. As we outline strategies for the modern individual, let's remember that the essence of resilience is ageless, though its application must continually adapt to meet the demands of our changing world.

Strengthening Emotional Resilience in Times of Change

Working through life's ever-evolving challenges requires emotional resilience. The volatility of the modern world, complete with its unique stressors such as constant accessibility, information overflows, and pressures of a high-performance ethos, means that our emotional fortitude is frequently put to the test.

Why Emotional Resilience?
First, let's set the groundwork by understanding what emotional resilience really means. It's not merely about facing challenges with a stoic face. Remember when we talked about high-performing teams? A group doesn't just succeed because they're brilliant; they excel because they have a shared vision, a collective passion, and an aligned action plan. Similarly, emotional resilience isn't just about individual strength—it's about understanding, managing, and expressing our emotions in a way that sets us up for success, both individually and collectively. Imagine, for a moment,

facing the challenging experience of being retrenched. The situation is fraught with uncertainty, mixed emotions, and a flood of questions about the future. In such a scenario, it's easy to feel disoriented and overwhelmed. But it is emotional resilience that enables us to navigate through this storm of feelings, to focus on the opportunities ahead, to maintain a positive outlook, and, most importantly, to fortify our determination to move forward and seek new beginnings.

The Connection Between Change and Emotional Resilience

Life is rarely a straight path. Every change, big or small, brings with it a whirlwind of emotions. It's quite natural. Remember those times when a sudden deadline adjustment or a shift in project direction caused a surge of anxiety? Or when a surprise appreciation at work filled us with elation?

We must remember that it's not the emotion itself but how we respond to it that truly matters. Emotional resilience is about absorbing, understanding, and managing these feelings, ensuring they neither cripple us nor lead us astray.

Strategies to Cultivate Emotional Resilience

To effectively deal with the constant barrage of changes and the emotional roller coasters they bring, it's essential to have a toolkit at your disposal. Here are a few strategies:

1. Mindful Reflection: Instead of getting overwhelmed by emotions, take a moment. Pause. Reflect. Understand the root of what you're feeling. Why not try practicing this in a cozy, informal setting instead of always battling emotions in high-pressure environments?

2. Seek Feedback Actively: Just as in collaborative brainstorming sessions where insights from colleagues can illuminate the way ahead, seeking feedback about our emotional reactions can provide invaluable perspectives. Sometimes, an external viewpoint can bring much-needed clarity.

3. Engage in Continuous Learning: Remember the satisfaction of achieving a set goal and the eagerness to then set a new one? Emotional resilience can be enhanced in the same way. Every emotional experience is an opportunity to learn, grow, and set new emotional milestones.

4. Practice Emotional Regulation: Recognize your emotional triggers, understand your default emotional responses, and focus on directing your feelings in a way that aligns with your broader life goals. This approach is essential for personal growth and achieving long-term objectives.

Embracing the Continuous Journey

Much like our discussions around dealing with stressors and nurturing competencies for future challenges, strengthening emotional resilience is an ongoing process. The more diverse our experiences and strategies, the richer and more robust our emotional resilience becomes.

In the face of change, armed with emotional resilience, not only do we remain steadfast, but we also rein in the power of emotions to move us forward, innovate, and reimagine possibilities. It's about making every emotional experience, good or bad, a stepping stone to a more fulfilled, content, and harmonious life.

Building Mental Resilience: Strategies for Flexibility and Adaptability

Ah, the mind—a fascinating swirl of thoughts, ideas, and emotions. Yet, in the wake of the world's dynamism, where uncertainties loom large and high performance is the norm, our minds, much like our emotions, are frequently thrust into the throes of challenges. The response? Developing mental resilience comparable to a masterful chess game, where strategic thinking, foresight, and adaptability to ever-changing scenarios are essential.

Strategies to Foster Mental Flexibility and Adaptability

While challenges and changes are inevitable, our response to them isn't. By nurturing mental flexibility and adaptability, we equip ourselves to respond rather than react. But how do we cultivate these skills? Let's explore some strategies:

1. Embrace Continuous Learning: Just as after achieving one goal, we ardently set another; similarly, our quest for knowledge should be insatiable. This doesn't merely refer to academic pursuits but extends to life experiences, diverse encounters, and even failures. The more we expose ourselves to varied situations, the more adept we become at handling them.

2. Practice Cognitive Reframing: Remember the last time a sudden change in project direction felt overwhelming? Instead of viewing it as a setback, could it be seen as an opportunity for innovation? Cognitive reframing is about shifting perspectives, turning challenges into opportunities, and obstacles into stepping stones.

3. Mindfulness and Meditation: Taking a leaf from our earlier chapters, mindfulness is not just a stress-relief tool. When practiced regularly, it fosters a heightened awareness of our thought patterns, allowing us to identify rigidities and actively work towards making our thought processes more fluid.

4. Engage in Problem-solving Exercises: Much like preparing well for a strategic meeting ensures its efficacy, regularly engaging in problem-solving tasks, puzzles, or even real-life challenges can bolster our brain's adaptability. Over time, it's not just about finding a solution but about enjoying the process of seeking one.

5. Build a Mental Support Network: Instead of only seeking guidance in formal settings, engage in casual brainstorming sessions, discussions, or even debates. Surrounding ourselves with diverse thinkers can often provide fresh perspectives, challenging our thought processes and thereby enhancing flexibility.

Mental resilience is not an isolated aspect of our being—it's closely connected to our emotional and physical selves. Every time we embrace change, adapt to a new situation, or even when we choose to take a break, refuel, and introspect, we are fine-tuning our mental resilience. The goal? To ensure that no matter what life throws our way, our selves work together in seamless harmony.

As we inch closer to the culmination of this chapter (and this book!), we must remember that our minds, much like a well-oiled machine, require regular maintenance. But instead of greasing gears or tightening bolts, our tasks involve constant learning, embracing diverse experiences, and cultivating a growth-oriented mindset. So, as we march forward, armed with strategies for flexibility and adaptability, let's also cherish each twist, turn, and terrain that this journey presents.

Cultivating Social Resilience: Nurturing Supportive Networks

In our journeys—be it professional, personal, or the intricate blend of both—we often underscore the significance of individual strength and perseverance. We discuss mental frameworks, emotional safeguards, and diverse techniques to stand tall amid storms. However, isn't it often said, "Together, we stand stronger"? The realm of social resilience echoes this sentiment, amplifying the symphony of collective strength.

The Element of Social Resilience

Consider the scenario of a community responding to a natural disaster. Individuals, each bringing their unique skills, hopes, and vulnerabilities, unite in response. The atmosphere is charged with a flurry of activity — planning, dialogues, disagreements, and solutions. In this collective effort, what grows stronger? It's the essence of social resilience.

The community's combined ability to recover from adversity is powered by mutual support and understanding. Social resilience goes beyond just having a network of contacts. It involves building a robust support system, a community where each member, reflecting the dynamics of a cohesive team, is united by a shared purpose, fosters enthusiasm, and advances with a strategic plan of action.

The Need for Nurturing Supportive Networks

In today's rapidly changing world, finding a nurturing haven is crucial. This safe space is often not a physical place, but a network of caring individuals. To appreciate its importance, one must consider the challenges that hinder personal growth. Reflect on those times when personal responsibilities, tight deadlines, or social

conflicts felt overwhelming. In such instances, the path to resolu-
tion is rarely walked alone. It is navigated through the nurturing
support of a community. This nurturing aspect within our networks is key. It provides more than assistance; it offers a sense of
belonging and mutual growth. Each person in this network contributes not just through their presence, but through their empathetic understanding and encouragement. Like a garden that
thrives under attentive care, these networks flourish, helping individuals and the group to overcome life's hurdles. In nurturing
these bonds, we foster an environment where collective strength
and shared wisdom lead to resilience and progress.

Crafting and Nurturing this Network: Strategies and Steps

Building a supportive network isn't an overnight task. It's a nuanced blend of identifying the right individuals, nurturing relationships, and ensuring mutual growth. Let's break this down:

1. Identify Core Members: Just as one would in creating a high-performance team, pinpoint individuals who align with your values,
challenge your perspectives, and bring diverse strengths to the table. These individuals form the core of your network.

2. Invest Time and Effort: Relationships, like plants, need consistent nurturing. Instead of engaging only in formal settings, create opportunities for candid interactions. Why not gather in a
comfy ambiance for a change, discussing goals, aspirations, and
shared challenges?

3. Establish Mutual Growth Pathways: Just as one would prepare
well before a strategic meeting, ensuring clarity of goals and alignment, do the same with your network. Understand what each

member seeks, and ensure that the relationship isn't one-sided. It's a symbiotic growth pathway.

4. Foster Open Dialogue: Think of the dynamic in a successful team meeting—where every member feels empowered to share their thoughts and ideas. This concept is equally vital here. Promote open, honest conversations, even those that might challenge the status quo. Such interactions are the ones that genuinely strengthen social resilience.

5. Engage in Collective Problem-Solving: Often, the most intricate challenges unravel when viewed through diverse lenses. Create avenues for group brainstorming, idea sharing, and collective problem-solving.

6. Celebrate Achievements, Big and Small: Just as after achieving a particular goal, there's an impetus to set another, similarly, in your network, celebrate milestones, big or small. It solidifies the bond and reinforces collective commitment.

The Influence of Social Resilience in Our Lives

Reflect on the moments when challenges seemed unconquerable. Now, reimagine these situations, but with a robust supportive network by your side. The landscape changes, doesn't it? Instead of solitary battles, you have a battalion. Instead of individual strategies, there's a collective game plan. And instead of singular celebrations, there is shared jubilation.

This is the transformative power of social resilience. It amplifies individual strengths, cushions vulnerabilities, and crafts a culmination of shared experiences, successes, and learnings.

Exercise: Creating a Personal Resilience Plan

Introduction: Ah, the beauty of resilience; like change, it contributes to your ever-changing future. We've thoroughly discussed each facet of resilience—mental, emotional, and social—and now it's time to put those discussions into action and create your personal resilience plan.

Objective: To design a holistic resilience blueprint that synchronizes emotional, mental, and social facets tailored to your unique needs, strengths, and aspirations.

Materials Required:
1. A comfortable, quiet space.
2. A notebook or digital device.
3. A calm, open mind.
4. A steaming cup of your favorite beverage, if you like (just to set the mood right!).

Steps:

1. Self-reflection: Begin with some introspection. Recall the challenges, changes, or choices that often tip your balance. Jot these down. This isn't a moment to dwell but a stage to recognize.

2. Identify Your Strengths: Think back to the moments of triumph and the challenges you've overcome. What inner strengths did you draw upon? Was it your emotional equilibrium, a flexible mindset, or the support of your close-knit network? Enumerate these strengths.

3. Establish Emotional Safety Nets: Recognizing that emotions can be turbulent, design your emotional safety protocol. It might be a mindfulness ritual, a particular hobby, or merely a serene spot in your home where you recalibrate.

4. Mental Flexibility Drills: The brain, much like a muscle, needs consistent workouts. Make a list of cognitive exercises, be it puzzles, strategic games, or even divergent thinking sessions. The goal? To keep that mental agility up and running!

5. Social Resilience Boosters: Now, this is akin to a team-building exercise. Identify key members of your support system. Plan regular check-ins, brainstorming sessions, or just candid coffee chats. Remember, the quality of interactions is what matters.

6. Continual Learning Agenda: Continual Learning Agenda: Recognize that, similar to the ongoing process of personal development, resilience is an ever-evolving journey. Develop a plan for continuous learning—select books to read, seminars to attend, or new experiences to undertake.

7. Review and Refine: Resilience, much like the strategies in a high-performing team, requires periodic reviews. Set a cadence—maybe quarterly. Revisit your plan, recognize what's working, and refine what isn't.

8. Celebrate the Journey: Just as after a successful project, pitch, or workshop, there's a moment of celebration, remember to celebrate your resilience journey. Cherish the milestones, learn from the bumps, and always, always look forward. Crafting a personal resilience plan isn't about creating a rigid roadmap. It's about laying down a flexible pathway, one that aligns with your individual rhythm, recognizes the changing nature of life, and ensures that through it all, your resilience is uplifting and uniquely yours.

With your plan in hand, you're not just prepared for life's challenges but are equipped to manage them with grace, strength, and an undying spirit.

Key Takeaways

- Resilience and change are deeply interconnected. As we react to change, we must activate resilience to regain balance.
- Human biology is an incredible machine designed to handle stress and promote resilience. Whether it's our brain's plasticity or our hormonal responses, our bodies have intrinsic mechanisms to bounce back. Yet, just as a high-performing team requires nourishment, so does our biological resilience.
- By strengthening our emotional core, we equip ourselves to face challenges head-on, be it a looming deadline or a sudden twist in our life's path.
- It's not just about mental strength but the agility to adapt, the flexibility to pivot, and the wisdom to discern. It's about pre-empting scenarios, strategizing responses, and refining our approach.
- Social resilience is our lifeline in a world fraught with uncertainty and constant accessibility. It's about creating spaces of trust, mutual growth, and collaboration, where together, we can tackle life's uncertainties.
- Crafting a resilience blueprint is much like preparing for a strategic meeting. Setting goals in a comfy atmosphere and designing a Personal Resilience Plan is a proactive approach. It's not a one-time strategy; it's an evolving blueprint that's often revisited and refined.

- *The Ultimate Insight:* Resilience isn't just about withstanding life's challenges but about evolving through them. Just as one doesn't stop after a single achievement but pushes forward, our resilience journey is continual, ever-evolving, and profoundly enriching.

Remember, as we move through this life armed with resilience, not only do we endure, but we thrive, we grow, and we transcend. Every challenge encountered becomes a stepping stone, and every change, an avenue for growth.

CONCLUSION

Thriving in the Ever-Evolving World

C hange, in its diverse forms, is an integral aspect of the human experience. It's a constant, ever-present in our lives, challenging, reshaping, and in many instances, enriching us. Through the preceding chapters, we've examined change from every angle—understanding it, embracing it, and, most importantly, thriving amidst it.

Reflections on the Journey of Embracing Change

In our exploration, we understood that change, while often daunting, is flush with opportunities. From the complex dynamics that impede improvement to the transformative power of forced shifts, we dove deep. We demystified Moore's Law, a beacon in this digital age, spotlighting the accelerated rhythm of technological advancements and how it's reshaping our existence. Throughout these chapters, a prominent theme emerged: the connection between change and resilience. It's a give-and-take relationship, each element complementing the other. Our emotional, mental, and social skills come together and create the resilience that's indispensable in these ever-shifting times. We also uncovered insights on artificial intelligence—a frontier of change that's redefining the contours of workplaces and societal interactions. While

AI's rise has sparked a spectrum of emotions, from awe to anxiety, it underscores a crucial message: that of the need to continually upskill and reskill as we sharpen our minds for the AI era.

Final Thoughts and Practical Steps for Sustainable Growth

Embracing change isn't merely about adaptation; it's about pro-actively seeking growth, even when comfort tempts us into stagnation. As we stand at this juncture, there are a few things to always keep in mind:

- **Awareness:** Recognize that information overload, deadline pressures, and uncertainties aren't just personal stressors; they're signals of change. Listen to them.
- **Mindset:** Move beyond the fear of the unknown. Recall our discussions on developing an open mindset. Be ready, be adaptable, and view change as a companion rather than an adversary.
- **Community:** The importance of nurturing supportive networks can't be emphasized enough. Lean into your community, foster deep connections, and remember that in times of change, there's strength in numbers.
- **Lifelong Learning:** The chapters on AI and embracing change spotlighted the indispensable role of continuous learning. Dive into workshops, leverage online courses, or simply engage in dialogues that challenge your viewpoints. Keep growing.
- **Action:** Lastly, it's pivotal to convert insights into action. Think about the exercises at the end of each chapter as a toolkit. Utilize them, refine them, and create a personal blueprint that resonates with your unique journey.

Exercise: Setting Long-term Goals for Personal and Professional Growth

As we close the book, it's only fitting that we take a moment for introspection. Let's visualize our future selves with one last exercise:

1. Reflect: Take a moment to think about the biggest change you've experienced in the past year. How did you respond? What would you do differently now, armed with the knowledge from these chapters?

2. Forecast: Anticipate a significant change on the horizon, either in your personal life or professional sphere. Jot down strategies inspired by our discussions to work through this impending shift.

3. Commit: Write down three long-term goals, both personal and professional. Ensure they resonate with the themes of embracing change and fostering resilience. Remember, specificity is key.

4. Check-in: Set a reminder for six months from now. When the time comes, revisit these goals. Reflect on your journey and the progress made, and recalibrate if needed.

That's it—we've come to the end of *The Power of Change*, but that does not mean that your journey has also concluded. We know that life is in constant flux, that change is always around the corner, and that we can and will find power in confidence, self-awareness, resilience, and adaptability. The future is ever-changing, and the time is now. It's all yours for the taking.

About the Author

Melissa's deep experience of working at the very top of global companies, combined with her extensive coaching skills and experience, has made her a highly sought-after coach and consultant for both current and aspiring leaders & teams. She helps leaders grow, stretch their vision and push their boundaries. She is greatly experienced at developing their skills so they can lead from where they are confidently and craft strategies that deliver change and real business re-sults with agility, pace resilience and consistency. Her specialty is partnering with her clients and providing tools to create action-oriented plans that drive their careers forward in a decisive manner. Melissa is a certified professional coach and member of the International Coach Federation. She is also a Fellow of the Institute of Coaching at McLean Hospital, an affiliate of Harvard Medical School, and a thought leader at Forbes Coaches Council. Her clients include those from large corporations, SMEs and startups. Melissa brings more than 20 years of business development & business consulting background and experience to her executive coaching practice. She grew up in Hamburg/Germany, lived in London/England, Singapore, Jakarta/Indonesia and commutes now between Vienna/Austria and Dubai/UAE. She is fluent in English and German and has first-hand experience of European, Asian and Middle Eastern cultures.

Printed in the USA
CPSIA information can be obtained
at www.ICGtesting.com
JSHW010240240124
55418JS00053B/278